Martin&Paul's surf

'n' turf

martin shanahan & paul flynn

photography by simon wheeler

contents

surf

martin shanahan

Ireland is probably one of the least polluted countries in the world. Our seas are not overfished, they are well-managed and clean. We don't have huge industry destroying the environment. The quality of our meat, seafood and dairy is magnificent. Travelling around the country to film Surf 'n' Turf has made me even more aware of the riches it has to offer. Going to places I have never been to before, travelling from Donegal in the north to Kerry in the south, I have found incredible delicacies, learned from master fishermen and met great characters. The dishes you will see in this book celebrate the quality of the brilliant Irish produce we found in every village and town we visited.

Paul and I are both chefs, but you won't find 'cheffy' food in this book. My style of cooking is all about respecting the fish; keeping it simple is the trick. And it's all about sourcing. When you are buying food, you have to get as close to its source as possible. If you can get to the quay to talk to the fishermen, then do so. Otherwise, go to the fishmonger who does that. Once you have got hold of the best – and with fish that means the freshest – everything else is simple.

At last, people are going back to the simple recipes and appreciating what's wonderful about home-grown produce. These days, we are not looking for expensive exotic or imported food, we want to eat local again. We are buying carrots at farmers' markets and fish down at the pier.

I want to show the Irish people how wonderful their own food is. Being on location, I have seen the surprise on people's faces when I tell them the ingredients I am cooking with are local. To make the show, we foraged for wild garlic and seaweed, or sought out organic sea trout, and you can do the same. Irish food is often exported even before it is landed, in the case of fish, which is great for the country, but it would be a tremendous shame if locals missed out altogether.

It's been a great pleasure duelling with my good friend Paul to create these recipes, and I hope you enjoy cooking from this book as much as we loved making it.

turf

paul flynn

We had a blast making Surf 'n' Turf. It was great to be out of the kitchen for once, and in the fresh air (well, the rain, mostly). The problem with chefs is that they spend their lives with their heads in pots. Meeting the people, as we did on the show, you get to know what they really want to cook and eat. It was all about getting out and about, finding the farmers that grow the food, and having fun. We cooked in underground fire pits, roasted meat on spits, even fished from kayaks!

Ireland is the best place you could be in the world when it comes to cooking with what you find around you. Where do you start when talking about the quality of Irish produce? With sweet, creamy Glenilen butter, or the salamis of Gubbeen charcuterie, smoked salmon from the Burren, or Crozier blue cheese...? With an Irish ice cream maker about to open a shop in Paris, Ireland is now truly on the world food stage.

But I want people to cook at home, too, and to learn how to take sensible short cuts. As the recipes here show, I'm all for making something delicious using ready-cooked food, or making bleakly unpromising veg the star of a dish. I love long, slow one-pot cooking with offcuts and pig's cheeks, where everything just melts together.

I've been cooking professionally for 30 years; making lunch and dinner with a quick break in the afternoon to see the children or snatch a power nap. For the most part I love my job, but I've got a dodgy ankle, I can be as bad-tempered as a bag of cats, and my wife wonders what I'm going to be like when I get older, as, indeed, do I. But I wouldn't swap this life for anything.

You see I'm obsessed with food, restaurants and all things culinary. The thrill of welcoming new ingredients that comfortingly appear with the seasons still excites me. The challenge of doing something special with them leaves me lying awake at night, staring at the ceiling.

Competing with Martin has been such great fun. He is always up for a bit of shenanigans. This book represents both our worlds, that in some ways are very different, though the love of good, simple, honest food resonates through both sets of our recipes. Enjoy.

1

starters and soups

crab claws, lemon, chilli and basil cream

Serves 2

500g crab claws, out of the shell
(fresh rather than frozen if possible)
1 x recipe Lemon Butter Sauce
(see below right)
3 tbsp sweet chilli sauce
handful of basil leaves, chopped

Crab claws that are sold out of their shells have already been cooked, so you'll only have to heat them through for this great dish

In a large, wide saucepan heat about 100ml of water to a boil, add the crab claws (they should fit in a single layer) and simmer for three minutes. Most of the water should evaporate; drain off any that remains. Toss with the Lemon Butter Sauce, sweet chilli and basil. Serve with steamed rice or French bread.

To make lemon butter sauce, heat 250ml of single cream in a saucepan to just boiling point. Gradually whisk in 80g unsalted butter, cubed. Add the juice of 1 lemon. Season with salt and white pepper, then simmer for 2 minutes. Avoid boiling, or the sauce may curdle.

creamy mushrooms on toast

Serves 4

4 slices of brioche
splash of olive oil
small knob of unsalted butter
2 handfuls mixed mushrooms, cut
so they are about the same size
2 shallots, finely chopped
1 garlic clove, crushed
pinch of a chicken stock
cube, crumbled
splash of double cream
sea salt
freshly ground black pepper
squeeze of lemon
handful of chopped parsley leaves
100g parmesan, grated

Old school and delicious, though not so good for the waistline. Try these with steak, too, or on their own as a light lunch.

Slice the brioche and toast it, then keep it warm.

Put the olive oil into a large frying pan over a medium heat and add the butter. When foaming, throw in the mushrooms with the shallots and garlic. Cook for a couple of minutes, until the juice starts to come from the mushrooms. Crumble in the stock cube and add the cream. Allow to reduce until the cream starts to coat the mushrooms, then season and add the lemon and parsley.

Serve the mushrooms on the brioche toast, scattering over the parmesan.

steamed dublin bay prawns, drawn butter

Serves 4

100g unsalted butter
1kg raw Dublin Bay prawns

So simple, yet so delicious. Today, Ireland is one of the largest producers of prawns, and the beloved Dublin Bay prawn is by far the most highly prized for its sublime flavour and firm texture.

In a small saucepan, melt the butter over a medium heat. Bring to the boil until the milk solids have separated and sunk to the bottom of the pan. Ladle out the clarified butter on top (discard the solids) and keep it warm until the prawns are steamed.

Place the prawns in a steamer and cook for three to four minutes. Remove and serve with a dish of the drawn butter.

baked camembert with spiced pears; pear, walnut and treacle bread

Serves 4

For the pears
225g caster sugar
300ml red wine
1 cinnamon stick
pinch of ground allspice
small piece of root ginger, grated
2 black peppercorns
1 fresh bay leaf
1 strip of organic orange zest
4 firm-ish pears, peeled, quartered and cored

For the bread
a little vegetable oil
250g strong white flour, plus more to dust
250g wholemeal flour, plus more to dust
2 tsp easy blend dried yeast
1 tsp salt
1 tbsp runny honey
1 tbsp black treacle
1 tbsp brown sugar
25g unsalted butter, melted
100g walnut pieces, lightly toasted
1 firm-ish pear, peeled and grated
coarse-cut oats, to sprinkle (optional)

For the camembert
1 camembert cheese
2 fresh bay leaves
freshly ground black pepper

A deeply satisfying autumnal dish. It's well worth making more spiced pears than you need, as they keep really well in the fridge (and the syrup is a very special addition to a glass of champagne or prosecco). None of this is difficult, though you would be best advised to make your spiced pears first, followed by the bread, then the baked cheese. If you don't fancy making the walnut bread you can always buy it…

For the pears, bring the sugar and red wine to the boil. Add the spices, bay leaf and zest and simmer for 10 minutes, then add the pears. Dampen a circle of baking parchment or greaseproof paper, scrunch it up, then re-smooth and place this directly on the surface of the liquid. Gently cook for 15 minutes, then allow to cool. (These can be prepared a day in advance.)

To make the bread, oil a 900g loaf tin. Put the flours, yeast and salt in a large bowl, add the honey, treacle, sugar and butter, then slowly pour in 250ml of warm water. Mix to a soft dough with your hands, adding a dash more water if it feels dry, then knead on a floured surface until smooth and elastic. (Alternatively, use a food mixer fitted with a dough hook and mix for five minutes.)

Add the walnuts and pear and knead briefly until evenly distributed. Put the dough in a lightly oiled bowl, cover with cling film and leave to prove for about 1½ hours, until doubled in size.

Punch the dough to deflate it, then tip it out on to a work surface. Shape into an oval, then drop into the loaf tin. Cover with cling film and leave to prove for a further hour until well risen. Meanwhile, preheat the oven to 200°C/400°F/gas mark 6.

Brush the top of the dough with water and sprinkle with a little wholemeal flour and the oats, if using. Score the surface with a knife, then bake for 30 minutes, until risen and golden. Turn the loaf out of the tin and tap the base, it should sound hollow (if necessary bake for a little longer). Cool on a wire rack.

For the camembert, preheat the oven to 200°C/400°F/gas mark 6. Take the cheese from its wooden box, discard the paper wrapping and push the cheese back into the box. Make two slashes in the cheese and push the bay leaves into the cuts, then season with black pepper. Replace the lid of the box and bake in the hot oven for 15–20 minutes (depending how ripe your cheese) until hot and bubbling. Serve with the spiced pears and the bread.

caramelised onion, beetroot and goat's cheese soup

Serves 4

2 tbsp unsalted butter
2 large onions, thinly sliced
1 garlic clove, chopped
1 sprig of thyme
2 raw beetroot, grated
330ml bottle of dry cider
750ml chicken stock
splash of balsamic vinegar
1 tsp brown sugar
sea salt
freshly ground black pepper
100g crumbly goat's cheese
edible flowers, to serve (optional)

What a colour! A beautiful soup for a high summer's day.

Melt the butter in a large saucepan and sweat the onions and garlic over a medium-high heat until nut brown in colour. Keep scraping the bottom of the pot with a wooden spoon to add colour and flavour to the soup. This process will take a little longer than you think, so be patient.

Add the thyme and beetroot, stirring to meld everything together, then pour in the cider and stock. Bring to the boil, then reduce the heat and let the soup simmer for 15 minutes.

Splash in the balsamic vinegar, add the sugar and season well with salt and pepper.

Divide between warmed bowls and crumble the goat's cheese on top. Sprinkle with edible flowers, if you have any, for a bit of glamour.

fishy fishy seafood chowder

Serves 6

100ml vegetable oil
500g raw prawn heads and shells
2 large carrots, chopped
1 large onion, chopped
100g tomato purée
2 garlic cloves, sliced
2 tbsp ground coriander
2 tbsp dried tarragon
100g unsalted butter
100g plain flour
sea salt
375g mixture of salmon
and firm white fish, chopped
200ml single cream

Give your friendly fishmonger a few days' notice and they'll keep the prawn shells and heads for you.

Heat a large saucepan and add the oil. Put in the prawn heads and shells, carrots and onion. Cook over a high heat for eight to 10 minutes, crushing the prawn shells as they cook. Add the tomato purée and three litres of water. Bring to the boil and simmer for 30 minutes.

Strain through a sieve, pushing as much of the prawns and vegetables through as you can for a rich broth, then add the garlic, coriander and tarragon and return to the rinsed-out pan over a gentle heat.

In a small bowl, make a roux by mashing together the butter and flour. Add this little by little to the hot prawn broth, whisking to thicken. Season with salt, then add the mixed fish and the cream, stirring gently so as not to break up the fish too much. Simmer for four minutes, then serve. You can add more cream and some white crab meat on top, if you want.

rockpool soup

Serves 4

50ml rapeseed oil
1 onion, thinly sliced
2 garlic cloves, thinly sliced
1 carrot, thinly sliced
4 tbsp tomato purée
stems from 1 bunch parsley
675g raw prawns, peeled
(keep the shells)
450g mussels
1 tbsp paprika
3 egg whites
1 bunch of dillisk (dulse) seaweed
1 bunch of sea spaghetti seaweed
1 bunch of chervil or flat-leaf parsley

This is a beautiful bowl of soup that looks just like a rockpool. It is important to have seaweed in it. You can use your own local edible seaweed, or get the real Irish deal online at www.spanishpointseaveg.ie.

Heat the oil in a saucepan over a low heat. Tip in the onion, garlic, carrot, tomato purée and parsley stems and cook until until soft, about five minutes. Add the prawn shells and the mussels. Pour in 600ml of water and add the paprika. Bring to the boil and simmer for 20 minutes. Strain the stock, then cover and refrigerate until cool. Shell the mussels and refrigerate them, too.

To clarify the stock, heat it in a large saucepan over a medium-low heat. Meanwhile, put half the prawns in a food processor. Add the egg whites and purée for about 30 seconds. Whisk this mixture into the stock and continue to heat, stirring gently, until it comes to the boil. Reduce the heat and allow to simmer. The prawn and egg white mixture should start to rise to the top and solidify. Allow the stock to simmer for 20 minutes. Now, gently break a hole in the prawn mixture, strain the consommé into a clean pot and keep warm.

Meanwhile, poach the remaining prawns, the dillisk and sea spaghetti in a little simmering water. The prawns are ready when they turn opaque and pink, and the seaweed just needs heating through. Reheat the mussels, too. Strain and add to the consommé. Serve in warmed bowls with the chervil.

oyster, creamed leek, smoked bacon chowder

Serves 4

100g smoked bacon, finely chopped
1 onion, finely chopped
2 leeks, finely sliced
600ml single cream
12 oysters (ask your fishmonger to
shuck them and save you the juices)
1 bunch of chives, chopped
sea salt
freshly ground black pepper
4 small sourdough loaves (optional)

Delicious: a creamy and decadent bowlful.

Heat a large saucepan, add the bacon and cook for three to four minutes over a medium heat, until the fat runs. Add the onion and leeks and cook for two minutes. Pour in the cream, bring to the boil, place the oysters in the pan with their juices and simmer for three minutes. Add the chives and season to taste with salt and pepper.

If you want to be a bit fancy with your presentation, scoop out the centre of the bread loaves, pour the soup in and serve immediately. Otherwise, just serve in warmed bowls.

slow-roasted shallots with serrano ham and mozzarella

Serves 4

good splash of olive oil
8 banana shallots, peeled and
halved lengthways
1 large sprig of thyme
sea salt
freshly ground black pepper
2 tbsp balsamic vinegar
2 balls buffalo mozzarella,
broken into pieces
8 slices serrano or parma ham

A great starter, these are also brilliant as a side dish with lamb, chicken or beef. I'm a great believer in making stars of humble ingredients, and the shallots really shine here.

Preheat the oven to 180°C/350°F/gas mark 4.

Place the olive oil and shallots in an ovenproof frying pan with the thyme. Season and roast for 15–20 minutes, until soft and golden. Add the balsamic, stir well and return to the oven for five minutes or so, until most of the vinegar has been absorbed.

To serve, tear the mozzarella apart, allowing three pieces per person (odd numbers always look better) and arrange on a platter. Spoon the shallots in and around, then drape the ham on top.

Shake the juices in the shallot pan to emulsify them, then drizzle them over the chunks of mozzarella and serve.

bacon and cabbage soup

Serves 4

1 onion, finely chopped
knob of unsalted butter
2 large potatoes, peeled
and chopped
600ml chicken or ham stock
4 bay leaves
1 small cabbage, shredded
sea salt
freshly ground black pepper
1 tsp English mustard
200g leftover cooked ham
or bacon, chopped
double cream, to serve
chopped chives, to serve

A new life for a classic combination. I never waste anything, and this recipe is meant to use leftover bacon, at the risk of having bacon and cabbage two days in a row.

In a large saucepan, sweat the onion in the butter over a medium heat, then add the potatoes, stock and bay leaves and bring to the boil.

Add the cabbage, then cook until both cabbage and potatoes are done.

Remove the bay leaves, then blend the soup until smooth with a little salt and pepper and the mustard.

Divide the ham or bacon between warmed bowls and ladle the soup on top. Serve with a swirl of cream and a sprinkling of chives.

creamed potato, warm clams

Serves 4

900g rooster potatoes, or other
floury potatoes
sea salt
200ml milk
100ml unsalted butter
freshly ground white pepper
50ml olive oil
1 onion, finely chopped
1 garlic clove, finely chopped
450g clams in the shell, washed
2 tbsp chopped flat-leaf parsley
1 bunch of rocket

My Irish version of clam linguine, but using the humble potato in place of the pasta! Discard any clams that are cracked, or that are open and do not close when firmly tapped.

Peel the potatoes, then chop into even-sized pieces and simmer in salted water until tender. Drain, then place in a mixing bowl. Meanwhile, heat the milk and butter together. Add to the potatoes, then whip together to a lighter consistency than that of mashed potato. Season and keep warm.

In a pan, heat the olive oil and add the onion and garlic. Cook for two minutes over a high heat, then tip in the clams. Cover tightly and cook for two minutes, tossing once (keep the lid on), then fold in the parsley.

Divide the creamed potato between four warmed bowls. Spoon the cooked clams and their juices on top. Sprinkle with rocket leaves and eat straight away.

salads

goat's cheese mousse with caponata bread salad

Serves 4 as lunch or a starter

For the goat's cheese mousse
1 sachet powdered gelatine
200g soft goat's cheese
275g crème fraîche
125ml double cream
1 tbsp runny honey
sea salt
pinch of freshly ground
white pepper

For the caponata
2 thick slices of white country bread,
torn into pieces
4 tbsp olive oil, plus more
for the bread
1 aubergine, finely chopped
1 red onion, finely chopped
1 tsp cumin seeds
2 garlic cloves, finely chopped
2 celery sticks, finely chopped
1 red and 1 yellow pepper,
deseeded and finely chopped
60ml red wine vinegar
2 tsp caster sugar
400g can plum tomatoes
1 tbsp capers
20 stoned black olives,
roughly chopped
freshly ground black pepper
½ bunch basil leaves, torn

This is one of my favourite things to have on the menu in summertime. If you don't fancy making the goat's cheese mousse, some grilled goat's cheese placed on top would be delicious.

For the mousse, dissolve the gelatine in a little warm water. Whisk the goat's cheese into the crème fraîche, making it as smooth as you can. In a separate bowl, whip the cream to soft peaks, then add the honey, salt and pepper.

Fold the goat's cheese mixture into the cream with the gelatine and chill for four hours.

To make the salad, preheat the oven to 180°C/350°F/gas mark 4. Bake the bread on a baking tray with a drizzle of olive oil until golden.

In a large frying pan, sauté the aubergine in half the olive oil until golden.

Remove the aubergine, then add the onion, cumin and garlic to the same pan with the remaining olive oil and cook for a further two minutes. Add the celery and peppers and cook for five minutes, until soft.

Add the vinegar, then the sugar and the tomatoes with their liquid and stir well. Cook uncovered for 10 minutes over a medium heat. Return the aubergine to the pan with the capers and olives. Season generously with pepper and warm through. Fold through the crispy bread and basil. Serve warm with a scoop of the goat's cheese mousse on the side.

cos lettuce, pears and blue cheese cream with hazelnuts

Serves 4

100g hazelnuts, almonds or pecans
150g medium-strength ripe blue cheese
200g crème fraîche
splash of good apple juice
a little sea salt
freshly ground black pepper
1 head of Cos lettuce, leaves separated and washed
2 ripe pears, sliced

Don't even think about using pears here unless they're properly ripe.

Place the hazelnuts in a dry frying pan, or on a baking tray in an oven preheated to 180°C/350°F/gas mark 4, and stir or cook, watching carefully, until toasted. Chop roughly and set aside.

For the dressing, put your cheese, crème fraîche, apple juice, salt and pepper into a jug and blend with a handheld blender until creamy.

Make sure the lettuce is dry and coat each leaf with the dressing as you would a Caesar salad.

Divide between plates, slice the ripe pear on top and scatter with the nuts.

warm wood pigeon, celeriac and cabbage salad

Serves 4

For the salad
25g hazelnuts in their skins
3 tbsp hazelnut oil
3 tbsp groundnut oil
1 tbsp white wine vinegar
2 tbsp sherry vinegar
juice of ½ orange
sea salt
freshly ground black pepper
2 leaves savoy cabbage, shredded
½ head of celeriac, peeled and cut into matchsticks
1 Granny Smith apple, cut into matchsticks
25g raisins

For the pigeon
1 tbsp light olive or sunflower oil
8 wood pigeon breasts
small knob of unsalted butter

Wood pigeon is a lovely introduction for those treading in unfamiliar game-cooking territory.

Make your salad first. Preheat the oven to 180°C/350°F/gas mark 4. Roast the hazelnuts in the oven, watching so they don't burn, then chop roughly.

Whisk your oils, vinegars and orange juice together, season and use to dress the cabbage, celeriac, apples, raisins and nuts.

Heat the oil for the pigeon in a frying pan until gently smoking. Place the pigeon breasts in the pan, skin side down, and cook for 90 seconds over a medium heat. Season, add the butter and turn over, turning off the heat as you do so. The meat should be pink and no more. Let the pigeon breasts sit in the pan for three minutes off the heat, covered with a plate, to rest and keep warm. Transfer to a chopping board and slice each breast at an angle. Serve on top of the nutty celeriac salad.

warm salad of cashel blue, apple and almonds

Serves 4

2 tbsp olive oil
1 tbsp unsalted butter
1 large red onion, peeled and cut into 8 wedges
2 apples, cored, each cut into 12
2 handfuls baby spinach or frisée lettuce, washed
250g cashel blue, broken into bite-sized pieces
2 tbsp whole blanched almonds
1 tbsp brown sugar
2 tbsp red or white wine vinegar
sea salt
freshly ground black pepper

This is a salad you would be happy to eat on a cold winter's day, with big hearty flavours.

Heat the olive oil and butter in a good heavy frying pan until foaming. Add the onion and apples, turning them when they start to colour. Meanwhile arrange the spinach or lettuce on four plates, dotting the cheese around.

Add the almonds to the onion pan, sprinkle over the sugar and shake the pan to coat everything evenly. Cook for a further two minutes, then pour in the vinegar and allow to bubble a little. When the apples are soft and golden, season well, spoon the mixture on to the prepared plates, dressing with the juices from the pan, and serve immediately.

warm salad of monkfish, butterbeans, semi-sun-dried tomatoes and oregano

Serves 4

2 tsp ground cumin
1 tbsp turmeric
1 tbsp ground coriander
500g monkfish fillets, skin and membrane removed
a little rapeseed oil
juice of 1 lemon
pinch of salt
200g cooked butterbeans
100g semi-sun-dried tomatoes
100ml sour cream
leaves from 1 small bunch of oregano, finely chopped
100g organic mixed leaves, washed

You can buy semi-sun-dried tomatoes in delicatessens, or at the deli counter of some large supermarkets, or you can even slow-roast your own in a low oven at home with seasoning, a little sugar and herbs (plum tomatoes work best).

Mix the cumin, turmeric and coriander in a shallow bowl. Roll the monkfish fillets in the spice mix, to coat evenly.

Heat a large frying pan and cook the monkfish in the oil for eight to 10 minutes, squeezing in the lemon juice and scattering with the salt at the end of the cooking time to give the flavours a lift.

Meanwhile, toss the butterbeans and semi-sun-dried tomatoes in a bowl, add the sour cream and oregano and mix well. Place on plates, slice the monkfish on top and serve with a mound of leaves over everything.

warm smoked mackerel, cherry tomato, green bean and red onion salad

Serves 4

1 tbsp French mustard
50ml red wine vinegar
1 tbsp caster sugar
150ml rapeseed oil
sea salt
freshly cracked black pepper
100g green beans
100g cherry tomatoes, halved
1 red onion, thinly sliced
4 smoked mackerel fillets

The onion and tomatoes really cut through the richness of the smoked fish here. A quick, refreshing and healthy lunchtime snack.

To make the vinaigrette, place the mustard, vinegar and sugar in a bowl. Whisk, slowly adding the oil. Season with salt and pepper and set aside.

Blanch the green beans in boiling salted water for three to four minutes, or until just tender, then plunge into iced water to stop the cooking and retain the beautiful bright green colour.

Place the cherry tomatoes in a bowl, add the drained green beans and red onion and toss together. Meanwhile, warm the smoked mackerel fillets under a preheated grill for four to five minutes. Place the salad on a plate, top with the warm mackerel and drizzle the red wine vinaigrette over everything.

fishy fishy seafood salad

Serves 4

For the red pepper dressing
2 red peppers
250ml mayonnaise (see page 136)
100ml white wine vinegar
60g caster sugar
1 garlic clove, finely chopped

For the parsnip chips
vegetable oil, to deep-fry
1 parsnip

For the salad
50ml rapeseed oil
600g mixed firm fish (salmon,
monkfish, gurnard, prawns), cut in
finger-sized pieces
4 tbsp sweet chilli sauce
1 spring onion, finely chopped
2 tbsp chopped coriander leaves
4 handfuls of salad leaves, washed
handful of parmesan shavings

At Fishy Fishy we just can't take this dish off the menu as it's one of our customers' absolute favourites. Make sure to ask your fishmonger to skin and bone the fish.

To make the dressing, preheat your oven to its maximum heat. Cut the peppers in half, place on a tray, skin side up, and roast until the skin blisters. This should take 10–15 minutes. When cool enough to handle, peel off and discard the skins and place the flesh in a blender with all the other dressing ingredients. Blend until smooth, then set aside.

For the parsnip chips, preheat the oil to 180°C (350°F) in a deep pan or deep fat fryer (you'll need an oil thermometer). Peel the parsnip, then remove crisp-sized shavings with a potato peeler. Deep-fry, in batches if necessary, until golden brown, being careful not to crowd the pan. Remove them from the oil with a slotted spoon, drain on kitchen paper and leave to cool.

To make the salad, heat the oil in a large frying pan. Place the fish in the pan and toss for two to three minutes until just cooked through but still juicy. Add the sweet chilli sauce, spring onion and coriander and toss again.

Toss the salad leaves in the red pepper dressing. Place in a bowl, then top with the warm seafood from the pan. Garnish with parsnip chips and parmesan shavings. Enjoy.

line-caught mackerel, pickled white cabbage salad

Serves 4

For the pickled cabbage salad
1 white cabbage, shredded
110g caster sugar
180ml white wine or cider vinegar
1 tsp sea salt
1 tbsp caraway seeds

For the fish
4 mackerel, filleted

Portmagee is famous for mackerel and there are few better ways to enjoy them than simply grilled and served with this salad. The pickled cabbage can be made a day in advance, covered and kept chilled. Return it to room temperature before serving.

Mix all the ingredients for the cabbage together with 100ml of water, the sugar will dissolve as you stir so there's no need to heat it. Set aside for at least four hours, for the flavours to mingle and mature.

When ready to eat, preheat the grill to its highest setting. Grill the mackerel fillets for three minutes on each side. Stir the cabbage salad to redistribute the flavourings, then serve with the hot mackerel.

warm lemon sole fillets, caesar salad and parmesan crisps

Serves 4

For the croutons
4 slices of white bread,
cut into 1cm cubes
3 tbsp extra virgin olive oil
pinch of salt

For the salad
1 large egg
1 garlic clove, crushed
4 anchovies
1 tsp Dijon mustard
3 tbsp red wine vinegar
1 tsp Worcestershire sauce
150ml extra virgin olive oil
3 tbsp lemon juice
sea salt
freshly ground black pepper
2 heads of romaine lettuce, outer
leaves removed, leaves separated
and washed
2 handfuls grated parmesan

For the fish
4 x 120g lemon sole fillets, skinned
100g plain flour
1 egg
300ml milk
150g white breadcrumbs
vegetable oil, to deep-fry

This is so good. Layers of crispiness from the romaine lettuce, the crumbed fish and the parmesan crisps all bounce off each other. It's especially popular with those people who tend to avoid caesar salad because of the anchovies, as the delicate, sweet lemon sole offsets them quite brilliantly.

First prepare the croutons. Preheat the oven to 180°C/350°F/gas mark 4. Toss the bread, olive oil and salt in a bowl. Spread out on a tray, place in the oven and watch carefully until golden brown. Remove and cool.

To make the dressing, place the egg, garlic, anchovies, mustard, red wine vinegar and Worcestershire sauce in a food processor. Blend together, then very slowly trickle in the olive oil. Add the lemon juice and season to taste.

For the fish, cut the sole into finger-sized pieces. Gather three broad, shallow dishes, In one, place the plain flour, seasoning it well. In the second, beat the egg with the milk, and in the third spread out the breadcrumbs. Dip the lemon sole fingers in flour, then turn through the egg mixture, and finally coat evenly in the breadcrumbs.

Heat the oil in a deep fat fryer to 190°C (375°F), using an oil thermometer to check the temperature. Cook the lemon sole fingers for six minutes, turning, until golden brown (you may have to do this in batches). Drain on kitchen paper.

Meanwhile, in a large mixing bowl, place the lettuce and croutons, then mix in the dressing and grated parmesan. Toss gently. Place in a salad bowl, top with the lemon sole and finish with Parmesan Crisps (see below).

For the parmesan crisps, line a small baking sheet with greaseproof paper and sprinkle grated parmesan cheese in 5cm circles. Bake in an oven preheated to 180°C/350°F/gas mark 4 for eight to 10 minutes until the cheese is melted and the crisps are golden. Remove from the oven and cool.

real man's salad

Serves 4

2 onions, thinly sliced
1 tbsp unsalted butter
1 sprig of thyme
200ml double cream
sea salt
freshly ground black pepper
8 rashers of streaky bacon, chopped
1 small black pudding, in 1cm cubes
1 tbsp vegetable oil
good splash of red wine vinegar,
or white wine vinegar
splash of olive oil
handful of leaves, such as red chard,
spinach and Cos lettuce, washed

*This is a salad dodger's salad, and came about almost as a joke.
A proper salad devotee called it 'a fry with a few leaves in it'. Maybe,
but it's tasty.*

Gently sweat the onions in a saucepan with the butter and thyme, without
colouring, until completely softened. Add the cream and reduce a little, then
season and set aside.

Fry the bacon and black pudding in a frying pan with the vegetable oil.
When nice and crispy, add the vinegar and olive oil to create a dressing.

Spoon the onion cream into warmed bowls, place the leaves in the
centre and divide the contents of the frying pan over the top.

roast duck, beetroot and watercress

Serves 4

For the dressing
50ml red wine vinegar
1 tbsp caster sugar
50ml sunflower oil
50ml olive oil
½ garlic clove, crushed
1 tsp Dijon mustard

For the rest
4 beetroots, peeled and quartered
2 tbsp olive oil
sea salt
freshly ground black pepper
sprinkle of thyme leaves
3 tbsp crème fraîche
1 tbsp creamed horseradish
4 cooked duck legs
2 handfuls of watercress, washed

This is all about buying good-quality cooked duck legs or half ducks. It's the easy option to get a great result.

Preheat the oven to 180°C/350°F/gas mark 4. For the dressing, bring the vinegar and sugar to the boil in a small pan, then allow to cool a little. Whisk in the remaining ingredients and set aside (keep whatever you don't use in the fridge for up to two weeks).

To make the salad, put the beetroots on a large square of foil with the olive oil, salt, pepper and thyme and roast in the oven for 30–40 minutes, until tender to the point of a knife.

Mix the crème fraîche with the horseradish.

Put the duck in the oven for 15 minutes, until reheated and crispy.

To serve, toss the watercress with the dressing and arrange a bed of it on each of four plates. Put the beetroot and duck on top, and drizzle with the horseradish cream.

smoked chicken and spiced pear salad with creamy blue cheese

Serves 4 as a starter

For the dressing
100g ripe blue cheese
100g crème fraîche
few twists of black pepper
a little good apple juice

For the salad
4 little gem lettuce, leaves
separated and washed
12 pieces of Spiced Pear
(see page 16)
1 smoked chicken breast,
thinly sliced
sprinkling of flaked toasted almonds

I do love smoked things, but not when they reek of smoke: subtlety, as in most things, is always the best approach. Simply double everything if you want to have this as a main course. You will have a little dressing left over, but that's all good. The dressing is all about the cheese. It has to be ripe. The better the cheese, the better the dressing.

Blend all the ingredients for the dressing well with a handheld blender or in a liquidiser, adding enough apple juice to make a light and creamy mixture.

Coat the salad leaves in the dressing. Arrange the pears on four plates, top with the leaves and scatter the chicken and almonds over the top.

3

quick

chickpeas with black pudding, garlic and parsley

Makes 4 tapas servings

2 tbsp sultanas
2 tbsp olive oil
½ large onion, finely chopped
1 garlic clove, crushed
1 tbsp pine nuts
1 small black pudding, finely chopped
400g can chickpeas, drained and rinsed
sea salt
freshly ground black pepper
handful of chopped parsley

This is a standby in our kitchen. It's a Spanish tapas recipe really, but it goes fantastically well with scallops, monkfish, chicken or pork. Mix in some salad leaves before serving, if you like, for colour and texture.

Soak the sultanas in hot water for 15 minutes, then drain.

Put the oil in a saucepan over a low heat, then sauté the onion and garlic until the onion is just tender.

Add the sultanas, pine nuts, black pudding and chickpeas and heat through, stirring all the time.

Season with salt and pepper, stir in the parsley and serve.

wokked mussels with sweet chilli and lime butter

This is a great dish for sharing, so place the wok in the centre of the table and help yourself.

Serves 4 as a starter

1kg mussels
60g unsalted butter
4 tbsp sweet chilli sauce
2 tbsp shredded root ginger
juice of 1 lime
2 spring onions, finely chopped
2 tbsp chopped coriander leaves

Wash the mussels well, pulling out the 'beard' from each. Discard any that are cracked, or that are open and do not shut when firmly tapped on the sink.

Place the mussels in a large pot with a tight-fitting lid, heave it over a high heat and steam for about two minutes, shaking the pan, until the mussels have opened. Remember, discard any mussels that do not open.

Heat a large wok or frying pan over a medium heat. Add the butter, sweet chilli sauce, ginger and lime juice. Cook for about two minutes, then add the cooked mussels, spring onions and coriander and toss everything together a few times.

Ready.

salmon with sticky honey-sesame dressing

Serves 4

For the dressing
100ml light soy sauce
50ml toasted sesame oil
2 tbsp runny honey
½ garlic clove, finely chopped
50ml rice wine vinegar

For the salmon
50ml rapeseed oil
4 x 200g skinless salmon fillets
sea salt
1 tbsp toasted sesame seeds

A dynamic dish, this is ready in a heartbeat. You have to be on the ball, but it means spending only minutes in the kitchen. You can use white wine vinegar instead of rice vinegar, if it's easier, but most people will have the other ingredients in their storecupboard.

For the dressing, place all the ingredients in a small pot. Bring to the boil and reduce until the sauce thickens enough to coat the back of a spoon.

Meanwhile, heat a heavy-based frying pan, add the rapeseed oil and allow it to get very hot. Season the salmon with sea salt on both sides, then place the fillets, presentation side down, in the pan. This will help achieve a nice crust on the outside and a moist texture on the inside. Cook for four minutes, then turn, cooking the other side for two minutes.

Place the salmon on warmed plates, spoon over the warm dressing and sprinkle with the sesame seeds.

five-peppered yellow fin tuna

Serves 4

1 tsp white peppercorns
1 tsp black peppercorns
1 tsp pink peppercorns
1 tsp green peppercorns
1 tsp red peppercorns
4 x 200g line-caught tuna steaks
finely grated zest of
½ unwaxed lemon
100ml crème fraîche
50ml rapeseed oil
2 handfuls wild rocket, to serve

In the spirit of surf and turf, I wanted to take on the peppered steak! This should be served medium-rare. Of course, you don't have to have all five types of pepper, but at least three would be good.

Place all the peppercorns in a spice or coffee grinder, or a mortar. Grind to a coarse powder. Place on a shallow dish, then roll the tuna steaks in the peppercorn mix. Mix the lemon zest with the crème fraîche in a small bowl.

Heat a heavy-based frying pan over a high heat, pour in the oil and allow it to smoke. Cook the tuna steaks for one minute on each side.

Place the tuna on warmed plates and drizzle over the lemon crème fraîche. Garnish with wild rocket and serve.

baked sea bream, tomato, coriander and lime salsa

Serves 4

For the salsa
2 ripe tomatoes, finely chopped
2 tbsp finely chopped red onion
2 tsp sweet chilli sauce
juice of 1 lime
2 tbsp chopped coriander leaves
sea salt

For the fish
4 x 180g sea bream fillets
50ml rapeseed oil

This is a healthy option, with no butter or cream in sight. Fresh fish is fantastic on its own, but responds very well to a bit of teasing from acid accompaniments such as this vibrant salsa.

To make the salsa, mix the tomatoes, red onion, sweet chilli sauce, lime juice, coriander, and a pinch of salt. Mix, cover and refrigerate for a few hours.

Preheat the oven to 200°C/400°F/gas mark 6. Place the sea bream, flesh side down, on an oiled roasting tray, season with salt and bake for 10 minutes until the skin is crispy. Remove from the oven, place on warmed plates and serve with the chilled salsa on top.

grilled whiting, mango, cucumber and lime salsa

Serves 4

For the salsa
1 mango
½ cucumber, deseeded and finely chopped
2 tbsp chopped coriander leaves
1 shallot, finely chopped
juice of ½ lime
2 tsp sweet chilli sauce
pinch of sea salt

For the fish
4 side fillets of whiting, each 180g
a little vegetable oil

Another variation on fish with salsa, this makes a lovely, simple summer dish.

To make the salsa, peel the mango and slice off the cheeks around the stone, then finely chop. Put all the salsa ingredients into a bowl and stir to combine. Cover and refrigerate for a few hours.

Turn on your grill to its highest setting. Place the whiting on an oiled roasting tray. Season with salt and grill for 10 minutes. Place on a plate and spoon the chilled salsa over.

pickled vegetables with quick pork rillettes and Irish charcuterie

Serves 6

For the pickled vegetables
1½ tsp coriander seeds
200ml white wine vinegar
100g caster sugar
1 piece pared unwaxed lemon zest
6 small carrots, sliced into coins on the diagonal
2 small red onions, cut into 5mm rings
12 baby gherkins

For the quick rillettes
300g cooked pork belly, chopped
1 tbsp Dijon mustard
splash of sherry vinegar
sea salt
freshly ground black pepper

For the charcuterie and bread
selection of salamis and cured meats (allow about 600g in total)
12 slices of crusty bread, or 6 rolls, or Melba toast, to serve
unsalted butter, to serve

A wow factor but with the minimum rattling of pots and pans. Rillettes are delicious on this all-Irish charcuterie plate, or they can also be spread on toast with chutney to great effect. You can use leftover pork belly to make rillettes, if such a thing exists…

To make the pickled vegetables, toast the coriander seeds in a small frying pan for a minute or two until aromatic.

Place the vinegar in a saucepan with the sugar, lemon zest and coriander seeds. Bring to the boil, then reduce the heat and add the carrots, onions and gherkins. Cook over a gentle heat for five minutes, then remove from the heat and leave to cool completely. These can be used straight away, or kept for up to two weeks in a sterilised jar. Drain well when ready to use.

For the quick rillettes, make sure the pork belly is at room temperature. Put all the ingredients into a food processor and pulse two or three times (no more) while scraping the sides to incorporate everything. Test for seasoning, then spoon into ramekins or kilner jars. Refrigerate for two to three hours.

Serve the rillettes with the pickled vegetables, charcuterie, bread and butter. Apple jelly and lightly dressed leaves will flatter the rillettes, as well.

warm black pudding bap with houmous

Serves 4

For the houmous
juice of 1 lemon
1 tsp caster sugar
400g can chickpeas,
  drained and rinsed
1 garlic clove, crushed
1 tbsp sesame oil
2 tbsp extra virgin olive oil
2 heaped tbsp crème fraîche
sea salt
freshly ground black pepper

For the baps
1 black pudding, sliced (you should
  have 12 slices)
4 soft baps

Sometimes things just don't sound quite right; this is one of those times. But trust me, the deep flavours of the pudding and the light creamy houmous work like a dream together.

To make the houmous, bring the lemon juice and sugar to the boil in a small pan, then allow to cool. Place in a food processor with the rest of the ingredients. Blend – I like to leave mine a little chunky – and season. (You could always add some fresh coriander, cumin seeds or chilli to this, to make it your own.)

Meanwhile, preheat the grill to its highest setting, then grill the black pudding on both sides until heated through and crispy.

Split the baps and spread each with 1 tbsp of the houmous. Fill each with three slices of grilled black pudding and enjoy.

warm corned beef sandwich with celeriac and raisin relish

Serves 4

For the relish
(makes 1 x 340g jar)
50g raisins
¼ head of celeriac
juice of ½ lemon
100g mayonnaise
1 tsp wholegrain mustard

For the sandwich
300g corned beef
8 slices good-quality sandwich
  bread, or 4 rolls, buttered

An Irish slant on the hot beef sandwich. (Corned beef = salt beef, depending on where you live.) If you haven't time to poach your own beef, buy it sliced from a good deli and reheat it. To cook it yourself, poach the meat for 30 minutes per 500g. To reheat, use a bit of stock or water, so the beef stays moist.

Soak the raisins in 100ml of boiling water.

Peel the celeriac with a serrated carving knife, then cut into 5mm slices. Grate it in a food processor, or on the coarse side of a box grater. Pour over the lemon juice and toss to prevent discolouration. Mix in the mayonnaise and mustard, then drain the raisins and stir them in, too.

If you need to reheat the beef, add a little stock or water and zap it in the microwave for a couple of seconds (it must be warm for this sandwich). Use the bread to make an open sandwich with the beef and serve with a generous amount of the celeriac relish.

spaghetti with crispy garlic, rosemary and chilli

Serves 4

500g dried spaghetti
2 garlic cloves, finely sliced
100ml light olive oil
good knob of cold unsalted butter
needles from 2 sprigs of rosemary,
finely chopped
sprinkling of chilli flakes
sea salt
freshly ground black pepper
lots of grated parmesan

We eat this all the time at home when there's nothing in the fridge, but never feel short-changed as it's full of flavour. Feel free to swap the rosemary for parsley, if you prefer.

Cook the pasta according to the instructions on the packet, then drain.

Meanwhile, cook the garlic in the oil over gentle heat until golden… it's important not to have the heat too high, or the garlic will turn brown and bitter and you'll have to start again. When it is golden, add the butter and rosemary and take off the heat.

Add the chilli flakes and fold into the spaghetti with a ladle of the pasta cooking water. Season and serve with the parmesan.

chorizo and parmesan garlic bread

Makes 1 baguette

100g unsalted butter, softened
3 large garlic cloves, crushed
fistful of chopped parsley
50g parmesan, grated
2 large slices of chorizo,
very finely chopped
1 small baguette

The old garlic bread idea pimped up with chorizo and parmesan. There's very little that can't be improved with chorizo, in my opinion…

Preheat the oven to 180°C/350°F/gas mark 4.

Mash the butter to a cream. Mix in the garlic, parsley, parmesan and chorizo. Slash the baguette evenly and stuff the butter into the slashes. Wrap in foil and seal.

Bake in the hot oven for 15 minutes, then unwrap the foil and serve piping hot.

butterbeans, chorizo and cider

Serves 4 as a tapas

1 onion, finely chopped
1 tbsp unsalted butter
5 sprigs of sage
1 garlic clove, finely chopped
1 tbsp tomato purée
1 tsp smoked paprika
100g chorizo, chopped about the
size of the butterbeans
100g black pudding, finely chopped
330ml bottle of dry cider
½ chicken stock cube
400g can butterbeans,
drained and rinsed
sea salt
freshly ground black pepper

This is me all over. I adore both butterbeans and chorizo.

Cook the onion slowly in the butter with the sage and garlic. When the onion is meltingly soft and sweet, add the tomato purée and smoked paprika and cook for five minutes.

Now tip in the chorizo and cook for a further five minutes, to allow it to release its oil. Throw in the black pudding and cook for two minutes, then pour in the cider, crumble in the stock cube and tip in the beans. Bring to a simmer and cook for a final five minutes. Season to taste, then serve on warmed plates, with crusty bread.

sautéed duck livers and serrano ham on toast

Serves 4

For the dressing
1 tbsp finely grated organic orange
zest plus the juice of 1 orange
1 tbsp crushed roasted hazelnuts
splash of balsamic vinegar
80ml extra virgin olive oil
sea salt
freshly ground black pepper

For the livers
plain flour
1 tbsp thyme leaves
500g duck livers, cleaned and
patted dry on kitchen paper
3–4 tbsp clarified duck fat or
vegetable oil
1 tbsp unsalted butter
2 large handfuls of baby spinach
4 slices of good sourdough toast
4 slices serrano or parma ham

Deeply savoury, rich and creamy. You can substitute chicken livers for those of the duck, of course. This might even tempt non-offal eaters.

Whisk all the ingredients for the dressing together and set aside.

Put the flour on a plate and season it well, adding the thyme. Turn the duck livers in the seasoned flour and pat off the excess.

Heat the duck fat until gently smoking. Cook the duck livers for about one minute on each side, or for a little longer if they are big.

Strain off the excess fat from the pan, then add your butter followed by your spinach, turn with the livers for 10 seconds, season and place on top of the warm toast.

Spoon the nutty orange dressing over and around, drape a slice of serrano ham over the livers and serve.

grilled organic sea trout, pappardelle, dillisk cream

Serves 4

4 x 200g sea trout fillets,
pin bones removed
200g fresh pappardelle pasta
30ml rapeseed oil
300ml single cream
50g fresh or dried dillisk (dulse)
seaweed, shredded
finely grated zest of
1 unwaxed lemon
leaves from 1 bunch chervil or
flat-leaf parsley, chopped

The taste of the organic sea trout grown in the clean, clear waters of the west coast of Ireland comes very close to my first memories of wild salmon. Feel free to use the edible seaweed found in your region, or get dillisk at www.spanishpointseaveg.ie.

Place the sea trout on a baking tray and grill for eight to 10 minutes.

Cook the pappardelle in boiling salted water with the rapeseed oil according to the packet instructions, then drain.

Meanwhile, bring the cream to the boil, then reduce the heat and simmer. Add the dillisk, lemon zest and chervil. Fold into the cooked pasta. Place in warmed bowls and top with the grilled sea trout.

megrim on the bone, semi-sun-dried tomato and lemon zest butter

Serves 4

100g unsalted butter
50g semi-sun-dried tomatoes
(see page 37)
finely grated zest and juice of
1 unwaxed lemon
sea salt
freshly cracked black pepper
4 medium megrim on the bone,
heads and fins removed

To me, megrim is a very underrated fish. It's from the sole family and can be cooked in the same way as dover or lemon sole. It is best grilled on the bone and makes a simple, easy supper.

For the sauce, gently melt the butter in a small saucepan. Roughly chop the semi-sun-dried tomatoes and add to the butter with the lemon zest and juice, salt and pepper.

Meanwhile, preheat your grill until very hot, and oil the grill tray. Grill the megrim, without turning, for 10 minutes; the skin should blister. Spoon the butter over the grilled fish and serve.

pan-fried brill, sugarsnap peas, hazelnut butter

Serves 4

100g unsalted butter, plus more to fry (optional)
1 onion, finely chopped
4 x 150g fillets of brill, skinned
vegetable oil, to fry (optional)
300g sugarsnap peas
1 tbsp caster sugar
50g whole hazelnuts, coarsely chopped (and some left whole)
juice of 1 lime
a little finely grated unwaxed lemon zest, to serve (optional)

Brill is widely available in the summer and is as good as turbot, but less expensive. It's always better to undercook fish than to overcook it, so give it less time than you think it needs. You can always cook it a little more if you really want.

In a frying pan, melt the 100g of butter and soften the onion slowly until sweet, but not coloured.

Simply grill or fry the fish fillets for a maximum of three minutes on each side, depending on thickness. (If frying, use a mixture of butter and oil.)

Meanwhile, add the sugarsnaps to the onions and cook for three minutes. Mix in the sugar, nuts and lime juice. Put the sugarsnaps on warmed plates with the brill on top, then spoon over the hazelnut butter and sprinkle with lemon zest, if you want. Enjoy.

crab, avocado and crème fraîche wrap

Serves 4

4 large flour tortillas
100ml crème fraîche
2 ripe avocados, peeled, stoned and sliced
300g fresh white crab meat
1 lemon

A quick and easy seafood wrap to give the old ham sandwich a run for its money.

Place the tortillas on four plates. Spread each with a quarter of the crème fraîche and avocado. Divide the crab between the tortillas and add a squeeze of lemon.

Roll it up, it's a wrap!

4

easy, slow or both

john dory in a magic bag

Serves 4

2 carrots, thinly sliced
1 large or 4 small roasting bags
4 x 150g John Dory fillets
250g asparagus spears
juice of 1 lemon
100ml olive oil
leaves from 4 sprigs of tarragon
sea salt
freshly ground black pepper

This is a great way of cooking fish while keeping the flavour intact. These bags are sold in all supermarkets for roasting poultry, but work really well with fish. Loads of people have said to me that they love eating fish, but don't cook it at home because it makes the kitchen smell fishy... well, here's your answer! Use a big roasting bag and cook all the fish together, or four small bags for individual portions.

Preheat the oven to 200°C/400°F/gas mark 6. Lay the carrots on the bottom of the roasting bag or bags. Place the fish on top. Slice the asparagus spears in half lengthways, mix in a bowl with the lemon juice, olive oil and tarragon and season well. Spoon over the fish, seal the bag or bags, place on a baking tray and bake in the oven for 12 minutes.

Remove and put on a plate unopened, opening the bag or bags at the table to enjoy the wonderful aromas from within.

coolea, potato and bacon bake

Serves 4

about 24 new potatoes
2 tart eating apples,
such as Granny Smith
2 pears
2 tbsp unsalted butter
400g streaky bacon, cut into chunks
sea salt
freshly ground black pepper
2 sprigs of thyme
1 tbsp brown sugar, or to taste
8 slices coolea, gruyère or
emmental cheese

This is just what you need on a cold evening, and not at all difficult to make. The perfect one-pot dinner. Use gruyère if you can't find coolea.

Preheat the oven to 170°C/340°F/gas mark 3½.

Halve the potatoes and cut them into chunks. Quarter and core the apples and pears and cut into slices lengthways; they should be about 5mm at the thickest part. Melt the butter in a heavy-based casserole and sauté the bacon and potatoes until golden all over. Add the fruit and turn it in the buttery juices. Season and add the thyme, with sugar to taste.

Cover with a lid and cook in the oven for 30 minutes or so, until everything is tender. You need to shake the casserole every so often to prevent anything from sticking, and add a splash of water if it is becoming too dry. When cooked, lay the slices of cheese on the hot mixture, then return to the oven for two to three minutes to melt.

Serve with a little dijon mustard on the side.

all-time simplest pork chops with apples

Serves 4

6 pork chops
2 red onions, quartered
6 potatoes, peeled, cut into chunks
2 apples or pears, quartered
glug of olive oil
sea salt
freshly ground black pepper
paprika, to taste
maple syrup, to taste
small firm black pudding,
cut into chunks
4 fresh bay leaves

A version of a tray bake, the apples melt into a sauce that gives us that magic old pork and apple sauce combo.

Preheat the oven to 200°C/400°F/gas mark 6.

Place the pork, vegetables and fruit in a large roasting dish. Pour over the olive oil, then sprinkle on the salt, pepper, paprika and maple syrup. Add the black pudding and tuck in the bay leaves. Put on a baking dish, toss with your hands and place in the oven.

Cook for 20 minutes, then toss everything in the tray again and cook for another 10 minutes or so.

Check that the potatoes are cooked, then serve.

roast duck with butterbeans and red chard

Serves 2 (or 1 if you are really hungry)

1 roast half duck or
2 confit duck legs
1 red onion, cut into 6 wedges
200ml red wine
1 star anise
1 tbsp redcurrant jelly
400g can butterbeans,
drained and rinsed
handful of red chard or baby spinach
small knob of unsalted butter
sea salt
freshly ground black pepper

I really believe if you make things simple people will cook more often, so I have based this dish on pre-cooked duck. The sauce is sort of a sweet and sour concoction that you can knock up really easily with a few ingredients from your larder.

Preheat the oven to 180°C/350°F/gas mark 4. Cook the duck for 15 minutes, or until crispy.

Meanwhile, put the onion, wine, star anise and jelly in a pot and reduce by half until a little syrupy.

Add the butterbeans, followed by the chard and butter, then season and warm through. Serve with the duck.

chicken, butternut squash, honey and ginger bake

Serves 4

A gooey, delicious dinner and a simple treat. Serve with a green salad.

8 bone-in chicken thighs
1 butternut squash, peeled, deseeded and cut into large chunks
2 red onions, peeled and quartered
1 garlic bulb, halved horizontally
good glug of olive oil
sea salt
freshly ground black pepper
1 tsp runny honey
1 red chilli, finely chopped
3cm root ginger, peeled and grated
3 sprigs of rosemary

Preheat the oven to 200°C/400°F/gas mark 6.

Place the chicken, vegetables and garlic into a large roasting tray. Pour over the olive oil and sprinkle with salt, pepper, the honey, chilli and ginger.

Mix everything together, ensuring it all gets a coating of oil and seasoning, then tuck in the rosemary.

Cook for 30 minutes, turning once or twice during cooking.

It is ready when the juices of the chicken run clear (pierce one of the fattest thighs right through to check) and the vegetables are soft and tender.

hake with salsa verde

Serves 4

For the salsa verde
1 garlic clove, peeled
small handful of capers
3 anchovy fillets
2 large handfuls flat-leaf
parsley leaves
leaves from 1 bunch of basil
1 handful mint leaves
12 pitted black olives
1 red chilli
3 tbsp red wine vinegar
8 tbsp really good extra virgin
olive oil
sea salt
freshly ground black pepper

For the fish
50ml rapeseed oil
plain flour
4 x 200g hake steaks

Hake is a very popular fish in Spain and one that has grown in popularity – deservedly – in Ireland over the last few years.

The best way to make salsa verde is to chop all the ingredients very finely by hand. Finely chop the garlic, capers, anchovies, herbs, olives and chilli and put them into a bowl. Add the vinegar, then slowly stir in the oil until you achieve the right consistency. Balance the flavours with a bit of salt (not too much because of the capers, olives and anchovies, so go carefully) and pepper. Set aside.

Warm a heavy-based pan and pour in the rapeseed oil. Allow it to get good and hot. Put the plain flour in a broad, shallow dish and season really well. Coat the hake steaks in the flour and tap off any excess. Place in the pan and cook for three minutes on each side. Remove from the pan and spoon over the salsa verde. How simple is that!

easiest lemon-rosemary chicken

Serves 6

12 bone-in chicken thighs
2 red onions, quartered
4 sweet potatoes, peeled and
sliced 1cm thick
1 garlic bulb, cloves separated
but not peeled
1 lemon, halved and sliced
good glug of olive oil
4 sprigs of rosemary
sprinkling of chilli flakes
sea salt
freshly ground black pepper

Truly, you need nothing with this, though a crisp salad would be lovely, or some simply steamed greens.

Preheat an oven to 200°C/400°F/gas mark 6. Mix all the ingredients together in an oven tray and bake for 30 minutes until golden, turning once or twice to keep everything moist.

Check the chicken is cooked by piercing the fattest thigh right to the centre; the juices that emerge should run clear with no trace of pink.

That's it!

baked pollock and fennel with a horseradish crust

Serves 4

2 fennel bulbs
300ml single cream
½ glass of dry white wine
4 x 180g fillets of pollock
(no skin, no bone, no fear)
100g unsalted butter
2 tbsp grated fresh horseradish
2 tbsp chopped dill
100g white breadcrumbs

I bet you never thought pollock could be this exciting.... If you prefer, you could cover the fish with the cream and wine sauce and pile on a thicker layer of the horseradish crust, baking the fennel naked in a separate dish... it's purely an aesthetic difference, and totally up to you.

Preheat the oven to 200°C/400°F/gas mark 6.

Finely slice the fennel bulbs. Place in a saucepan and cover with the cream and white wine. Bring to the boil.

Place the fish in an ovenproof dish. Pour over the fennel, cream and wine.

To make the crust, melt the butter in a pot. Add the horseradish, dill and breadcrumbs. Mix together, then spread evenly on top of the fish and fennel. Bake in the hot oven for 15 minutes, then serve.

thai-style ling curry

Serves 4

1 onion, finely chopped
2 garlic cloves, finely chopped
50ml vegetable oil
4 tbsp yellow Thai curry paste
1 thumb-size piece of root ginger,
finely grated
400g can good-quality coconut milk
2 tbsp Thai fish sauce
2 tbsp brown sugar, or to taste
600g ling fillets, skinned and boned
generous handful coriander leaves
4 spring onions, finely sliced
juice of 2 limes

*Ling is a great – and sustainable – alternative to cod and monkfish.
Meaty and firm, it holds together really well in a curry.*

To make the sauce, sweat off the onion and garlic in a saucepan with the
oil until soft but not coloured. Add the curry paste and ginger. Cook for
two minutes, then add the coconut milk, 300ml of water and the fish sauce.
Bring to the boil, reduce the heat and simmer for 15 minutes.

Now add the brown sugar and taste. When the sauce is ready, cut the fish
into 5cm pieces. Gently fold the fish into the sauce and simmer for a final five
minutes, until just cooked through. Sprinkle with the coriander and spring
onions and squeeze over the lime juice.

Serve with steamed rice.

peach and smoky bacon chutney

Makes 3 x 340g jars

2 x 420g cans of peaches in juice
½ small onion, finely chopped
1 tsp curry powder
½ tsp mustard seeds
½ tsp turmeric
1 tbsp demerara sugar
2 rashers of smoked bacon, finely chopped
100ml white wine vinegar
1 tbsp cornflour

I serve this with a crumbly hunk of mature cheddar cheese. It is certainly unusual, but it's the business.

Drain and chop the peaches, reserving the juice.

Put all the ingredients except the cornflour – including the peach juice – into a large pot. Bring to the boil and simmer gently for 20 minutes. Slake the cornflour with a little water until smooth, add to the pot and cook for five more minutes to thicken.

Cool, then pot in sterilised jars. It will keep for three weeks in the fridge.

lamb and sweet potato supper

Serves 4

8 lamb chops
3 sweet potatoes, peeled and cut into large chunks
2 red onions, peeled and quartered
1 garlic bulb, cloves separated but not peeled
good glug of olive oil
sea salt
freshly ground black pepper
1 tsp cumin seeds
1 tsp brown sugar
sprinkling of chilli flakes
3 sprigs of rosemary

I grew up with a lot of boiled food. I have no problem with it, but when you boil something all the goodness and flavour just disappears into the cooking water. With tray bakes such as this, all the ingredients intermingle and caramelise and the flavours concentrate. Plus the washing-up is kept to a minimum, a very important part of cooking in my view...

Preheat the oven to 200°C/400°F/gas mark 6.

Place the lamb, vegetables and garlic into a large roasting tray and pour over the olive oil. Sprinkle on salt, pepper, the cumin, sugar and chilli flakes. Mix everything together, ensuring it all gets a coating of the oil and seasonings. Tuck in the rosemary.

Cook for 30 minutes, turning once or twice during cooking. It is ready when the lamb is tender and the vegetables soft. You will have some crunchy, crispy bits, all this will make the dish better.

wild rabbit in cider and buttermilk with kale

Serves 2

2 tbsp unsalted butter
1 onion, finely chopped
1 garlic clove, crushed
small knob of root ginger, peeled
and finely chopped
¼ orange-fleshed turnip (swede, if
you're English), finely chopped
1 wild rabbit, skinned and jointed
1 tbsp plain flour
500ml chicken stock
330ml bottle of dry cider
1 large sprig of thyme
handful of kale, well washed
and shredded
200ml buttermilk
sea salt
freshly ground black pepper
pinch of caster sugar

This is rustic one-pot food at its best: slow, deep but vibrant. Farmed rabbit or chicken would be a perfect substitute.

Place the butter, onion, garlic, ginger and turnip into a deep pot and start to sweat over a moderate heat. The onions should soften, but not colour.

Add the rabbit shoulders and legs along with the flour and stir into the softened vegetables. Cover with the stock and cider and tuck in the thyme, then simmer for 20 minutes.

Now add the rabbit saddle, which needs less cooking than the shoulders and legs, and cook for a further 20–30 minutes until everything is tender, then add the kale, buttermilk, salt, pepper and sugar. Stir together and return to a simmer for all the flavours to amalgamate.

Serve with rice or mashed potatoes.

5

comforting

christy hurley's crab crumble

**Serves 4 as a starter,
or 2 for supper**

4 tbsp chopped parsley
100g white breadcrumbs
50ml olive oil
450g fresh white crab meat
1 recipe Lemon Butter Sauce
(see page 11)

Christy is one of three generations of his family of fishermen who supply us at Fishy Fishy Café. This makes a great dinner party starter, as well as a comforting supper dish for two, with crusty bread.

Preheat the oven to 220°C/425°F/gas mark 7.

Mix together the parsley, breadcrumbs and olive oil in a bowl for the crumble topping.

To assemble the dish, divide the crab meat between four shallow bowls for a starter, or two for a supper. Cover with the Lemon Butter Sauce and top with the parsley breadcrumbs.

Place in the hot oven for eight to 10 minutes, until the breadcrumb mix has browned and the crab meat heated through, then serve.

fondue of cheddar and chives with crispy bacon, broccoli and new potatoes

Serves 4

For the bits and pieces
16 small new potatoes
sea salt
12 rashers of streaky bacon
good handful of broccoli florets
extra virgin olive oil

For the fondue
4 egg yolks
200ml apple juice
generous handful of grated mature
cheddar cheese
1 tbsp Dijon mustard
a little freshly grated nutmeg
freshly ground black pepper
1 tbsp chopped chives

I love fondues, and the whole lazy grazing vibe. Here, I give cheese fondue a bit of a twist by making it with a whisked cheese sabayon, further lightened with apple juice, and flavoured with chopped chives. (Incidentally, this sabayon also makes a wonderful pasta sauce.)

Cook the potatoes in boiling salted water for 15 minutes, or until tender to the point of a knife, then drain.

Cook the bacon in a large frying pan in its own fat, turning, until crisp. Remove from the heat and leave to drain on kitchen paper.

To blanch the broccoli, place the florets in a large pot of boiling salted water. When just cooked but still a little crisp, scoop out, then plunge into iced water to stop the broccoli overcooking and keep the lovely green colour, then drain well.

For the fondue, put the egg yolks and apple juice in a bowl over a pot of gently simmering water. It's important not to let the water touch the bowl, we need the steam to cook the eggs. With an electric whisk, whisk for seven to eight minutes, until trebled in volume, light and creamy. Fold in the cheese, mustard, nutmeg, salt, pepper and chives and keep warm.

To serve, place the broccoli, potatoes and bacon on a platter. Drizzle with some olive oil and scatter over some sea salt and pepper. Serve the fondue sauce in a warmed bowl.

smoky maple baked beans

Serves 4–6

glug of olive oil
2 garlic cloves, finely sliced
knob of unsalted butter
4 thick slices of smoked bacon,
  finely chopped
2 celery sticks, finely chopped
1 sprig of thyme
1 large onion, finely chopped
1 tbsp tomato purée
1 glass of dry cider
400g can chopped tomatoes
400g can butterbeans,
  drained and rinsed
400g can red kidney beans,
  drained and rinsed
2 tbsp maple syrup
sea salt
freshly ground black pepper

This is simply one of my favourite things to cook and eat. I love butterbeans, but the deep favours of this dish are beguilingly moreish either on their own or with roasted white fish, chicken or lamb. If you don't want to have two types of beans (though the kidney beans look dramatic in the mix), just use two cans of butterbeans instead.

Heat the oil over a gentle heat and add the garlic. Carefully cook until golden, but no more, to give a roasted garlic oil; if you take it too far, the garlic will burn and become bitter, and you'll have to start again.

Add the butter, bacon, celery, thyme and onion, then cook slowly for 15 minutes until soft and sweet. Add the tomato purée, cider and chopped tomatoes. Finally, add both types of beans.

Cook for five more minutes to heat through, then stir in the maple syrup, season well with salt and pepper and serve.

potato, turnip and prune gratin

**Serves 4 as supper,
or 8 as a side dish**

200ml milk
400ml double cream
1 garlic clove, finely chopped
freshly grated nutmeg
6 large potatoes, peeled
1 orange-fleshed turnip (swede, if
  you're English), peeled
sea salt
freshly ground black pepper
10 prunes, halved

I love prunes and turnips together, and this is a delicious gratin. It's lovely on its own as a vegetarian supper, with the bitter turnip and sweet prunes elevating the humble potato gratin to unusual heights. You can serve it as a side dish too, it's great with Roast Guinea Fowl (see page 114), or with lamb or pork chops.

Put the milk, cream, garlic and nutmeg into a large stainless-steel pot and bring to the boil.

Thinly slice the potatoes and turnip on a mandolin, or with a very sharp knife, and add to the milk and cream mixture. Season well and cook over a gentle heat until the potatoes are almost tender. Meanwhile, preheat the oven to 160°C/325°F/gas mark 3.

Check the seasoning, then place half the vegetables in a gratin dish. Add a layer of prunes, then top with the remaining potato and turnip mixture.

Bake in the oven for 15–20 minutes, then serve.

braised pork cheeks, warm leek and potato salad

Serves 4

For the cheeks
1 tbsp sunflower oil
2 tbsp unsalted butter
a little plain flour, to dust
sea salt
freshly ground black pepper
12 pork cheeks
1 onion, finely chopped
1 carrot, finely chopped
1 celery stick, finely chopped
1 garlic clove, crushed
1 sprig of thyme
1 rasher of bacon, finely chopped
330ml bottle of ale
½ chicken stock cube (optional)
pinch of caster sugar, to taste

For the potato salad
75g unsalted butter
1 leek, white part only, well washed
and very finely chopped
½ tbsp plain flour
12 new potatoes, cooked, peeled,
and roughly chopped
1 tbsp Dijon mustard
sprinkle of thyme leaves

Pork cheeks are delicious delicacies, tender, sticky, packed full of flavour and reasonably priced. Your butcher should be able to get you some if you ask him ahead of time. If they prove difficult to find, you can use chunks of pork shoulder instead, just get your butcher to take off all the skin, trim the fat and cut it into 7.5cm chunks.

Preheat the oven to 160°C/325°F/gas mark 3.

Put half the oil and half the butter into a casserole and place on the stove over a medium heat.

Put the flour into a shallow dish and season it well. Turn the cheeks in the flour and pat off the excess. Place them in the bubbling fat, brown on both sides, then remove from the pan.

Tip out the used fat and wipe the pan, then add the rest of the oil and butter followed by the vegetables. Brown these gently, then add the garlic, thyme and bacon. Return the cheeks to the pot and pour the beer on top. If the beer doesn't cover the meat and vegetables, add a little water and crumble in the stock cube. Cover and place in the oven for 1¼ hours. The cheeks should be very soft, but if they need a little more time, don't panic.

When the cheeks are soft, remove from the oven. Take the meat out of the casserole with a slotted spoon and keep warm. Strain the juices through a sieve into a saucepan, being sure to give the vegetables a good press down with a ladle, to get all their flavours into the sauce. Reduce your juices until nice and syrupy, taste and season, adding the sugar if they seem a little bitter.

Meanwhile, to make the potato salad, melt the butter, add the leek and sweat for three minutes over a gentle heat until they start to soften. Sprinkle over 3 tbsp of water, followed by the flour. Cook for a further two minutes, then fold in the potatoes, mustard, salt, pepper and thyme.

Return the cheeks to their reduced juices and check for seasoning.

Serve the leek and potato salad immediately in warmed bowls, with the pork cheeks and juices on top.

skate with cockles, mussels and guinness cream

Serves 4

rapeseed oil
plain flour, to coat
sea salt
freshly ground black pepper
4 x 200g skate wings
50g unsalted butter
1 onion, finely chopped
100g cockles in the shell, scrubbed
100g mussels in the shell, scrubbed
100ml single cream
300ml bottle of Guinness
1 tbsp chopped chives

A dish in honour of Dublin. Skate is hugely popular there, we all know the song about Molly Malone and her cockles and mussels, and of course Guinness is brewed there, too. Remember, don't eat any shellfish whose shells remain closed after they've been cooked.

Heat two large frying pans over a high heat. Add the rapeseed oil. Put the flour in a broad, shallow dish and season well. Dip the skate in the flour, then shake off the excess and cook for five minutes on each side.

Meanwhile, prepare the sauce. Heat a saucepan, add the butter and onion and cook for two minutes. Then add the cockles and mussels, cream and Guinness. Cover with a tight-fitting lid and cook for two minutes, until the shells are open. Place the skate on hot plates and spoon over the cockles, mussels and Guinness cream. Sprinkle with the chives and serve.

special roast potatoes with polenta, chorizo, goose fat, garlic and thyme

Serves 4

8–10 potatoes, peeled
3 tbsp polenta (coarse or fine)
3 tbsp goose fat
200g chorizo, in 2cm cubes
1 sprig of thyme
1 garlic bulb, cloves separated
but not peeled
sea salt
freshly ground black pepper
2 knobs of unsalted butter

These are our Sunday roast and Christmas Day potatoes. You can of course omit the chorizo, but what's a little extra pork between friends? A sprinkling of smoked paprika added at the beginning would be amazing on these potatoes, if you have it.

Preheat the oven to 200°C/400°F/gas mark 6.

Boil or steam the potatoes until just tender, then drain and allow to cool a little. Break and cut them into a large tray to get different, interesting shapes, then coat with the polenta, shaking.

Heat the goose fat in a roasting dish or ovenproof frying pan. When hot, add the potatoes, chorizo, thyme and garlic.

Season and put in the oven with the butter. Cook for 20–25 minutes, turning once or twice, until golden and crispy.

roast guinea fowl with cider butter, sage and brussels sprouts

Serves 2

1 guinea fowl
2 tbsp Dijon mustard
sea salt
freshly ground black pepper
3 onions, quartered
2 sprigs of sage
2 rashers of smoked bacon,
roughly chopped
good knob of unsalted butter
750ml dry cider
12 Brussels sprouts, halved
1 tbsp apple jelly

I love one-pot cooking, for I am, in my natural state, a lazy man. Of course you can substitute chicken for the guinea fowl if you wish.

Preheat the oven to 180°C/350°F/gas mark 4.

Rub the guinea fowl with the mustard and sprinkle with salt and pepper. Place the onions in a deep ovenproof pot. Add the guinea fowl, sage, bacon and butter, pour around the cider and bring to the boil. Cover with a lid and cook in the oven for one hour.

Add the sprouts and return to the oven for 20 minutes, this time with the lid off.

Remove the guinea fowl, sprouts, onions and bacon and keep warm. Add the apple jelly to the juices and reduce until slightly syrupy. Carve the bird and serve with the bacon, sprouts and onions. Drizzle with the pan juices. This is delicious with Potato, Turnip and Prune Gratin (see page 106).

roast cod, savoy cabbage, crispy gubbeen bacon

Serves 4

2 tbsp rapeseed oil, plus more for
the cabbage
1 onion, finely chopped
1 savoy cabbage, shredded
sea salt
freshly ground white pepper
4 x 200g sustainably stocked cod
steaks (no skin, no bone, no fear)
4 rashers of Gubbeen bacon, or
other good-quality dry-cured bacon
200ml single cream
80g unsalted butter

*A fabulous combination. I love any fish or seafood with bacon, and the
soft yet firm texture of the cod here is great with the crispy bacon.*

Preheat your oven to 200°C/400°F/gas mark 6. In a pot, sweat the onion
in a little oil for about two minutes. Add the cabbage and about 100ml of
water. Stir and simmer for eight minutes. By this time the water will have
evaporated (though drain off any that remains).

Meanwhile, heat the 2 tbsp of rapeseed oil in an ovenproof pan on the
hob. Season the cod steaks. Place in the pan and brown for a minute on each
side. Cover with foil and place in the hot oven for eight minutes. At the same
time, put the bacon on a roasting tray in the oven.

Add the cream and butter to the cabbage and simmer for four minutes
more. Place it on warmed plates with the cod and crisp bacon on top.

red gurnard, spring onion mash, lemon butter sauce

Serves 4

For the spring onion mash
1kg rooster potatoes
200ml milk
100g unsalted butter
3 spring onions, finely chopped
sea salt
freshly ground black pepper

For the rest
50g plain flour
8 red gurnard fillets, skinned and
boned by your fishmonger
a little vegetable oil
1 recipe Lemon Butter Sauce
(see page 11)

*Gurnard used to be a bait fish. What a waste! Because it lives on the
seabed, it eats a lot of crab, and you can really taste that in the flesh.
Fish and potatoes is the ultimate comfort food.*

To make the spring onion mash, peel and chop the potatoes. Place in a pot,
cover with water and boil for 20 minutes. Heat the milk and butter, then add
the spring onions. Drain the potatoes, then mash and add the milk and spring
onions. Season with salt and pepper.

For the gurnard, sprinkle the flour on a plate and season well with salt
and pepper. Coat the fish in the flour, tapping off any excess to avoid burning
it in the pan. Heat the oil in a large frying pan until hot, then fry the fillets for
four minutes on each side while you warm through the Lemon Butter Sauce.
Serve the fish with the mash and sauce.

finbar's smoked haddock, sea spinach and potato gratin

Serves 4 as a light supper

150g undyed smoked haddock
a few slices of onion
1kg waxy potatoes
50g unsalted butter, plus more
for the dish
100g sea spinach, or
normal spinach
sea salt
freshly ground black pepper
500ml single cream

I pick sea spinach (aka sea beet) in April, May and June all along the coast of west Cork. For this dish we use Finbar Desmond's natural smoked haddock which he catches and smokes himself in Kinsale. Finbar is one of the forward-thinking fishermen of his generation.

Poach the smoked haddock in simmering water with the onion for four to five minutes. Drain and cool.

Preheat the oven to 160°C/325°F/gas mark 3. Peel the potatoes and cut them into slices about the thickness of a coin (use a mandolin, if you have one). Butter an ovenproof dish and layer in the potatoes, haddock and sea spinach. Season lightly with salt and black pepper as you go, and finish with a neat layer of potatoes.

Pour over the cream, dot with butter and bake for 1½ hours, at which point the sea spinach, potatoes and smoked haddock should be melting into the cream. A great supper dish.

braised lamb shanks with garlic, rosemary and butterbeans

Serves 4

I like to serve this with celeriac mashed potatoes, to mop up the juices.

2 carrots
2 celery sticks
1 leek
2 small onions
plain flour, to dust
sea salt
freshly ground black pepper
4 lamb shanks
2 tbsp duck fat or olive oil,
plus a little more
4 garlic cloves
2 good sprigs of flat-leaf parsley,
plus ½ bunch, chopped, to serve
1 bay leaf
½ bottle red wine
400ml chicken stock or water
400g can butterbeans,
drained and rinsed

Preheat the oven to 160°C/325°F/gas mark 3.

Cut the carrots, celery, leek and onions into relatively even 2cm chunks.

Put some flour in a broad, shallow dish, and season it well with salt and pepper. Turn the shanks in the seasoned flour to coat, then pat off the excess. Heat the duck fat or oil in a casserole over a medium heat, then fry the lamb, turning, until golden and crispy. Remove from the casserole and set aside.

Drain off the excess fat and add some fresh oil. Add the carrots, celery, leek, onions, garlic, sprigs of parsley and bay leaf and cook over a high heat until the vegetables are browned.

Deglaze the casserole by adding the red wine, scraping the residue on the bottom of the pan and stirring well. Add the stock or water, place the shanks on top of the vegetables, cover and cook in the oven for 2½ hours.

When the lamb is cooked, skim the fat from the top of the sauce, add the butterbeans and chopped parsley, and season to taste. Place over a medium heat until just heated through, then serve.

crispy fried rock salmon with smoked paprika and sweet garlic aïoli

Serves 4

For the aïoli
300ml extra virgin olive oil
4 garlic cloves
2 egg yolks, plus 1 whole egg
2 tsp English mustard
1 tsp smoked paprika
2 tsp white wine vinegar

For the fish
vegetable oil, to deep-fry
300ml buttermilk
150g plain flour
pinch of sea salt
freshly ground black pepper
600g rock salmon (dogfish) fillets,
cut into finger-sized pieces
lemon wedges, to serve

Aïoli is a fancy word for garlic mayonnaise. Here, olive oil gives it a rich flavour, while the smoked paprika really enhances the fish.

Bring the olive oil to a very gentle simmer in a small saucepan. Throw in the garlic and simmer in the olive oil for three to four minutes. Cool it down, then scoop out the garlic.

Now, in a food processor, place the garlic, egg yolks and whole egg and mustard and blend until smooth. Slowly add the cooled olive oil in a very, very gentle trickle until it forms a smooth sauce. You really do have to go slowly here, or the aïoli might split. Add the smoked paprika and white wine vinegar. Set aside.

For the rock salmon, heat the oil in your deep-fat fryer to 190°C (375°F). (You should use an oil thermometer for this.) Put the buttermilk and the flour in two separate broad dishes, seasoning the flour well. Turn the fish in the buttermilk, lift out, then roll in the flour. Pat off the excess, then deep-fry in the oil for four minutes. (You may have to fry in batches, to avoid crowding the pan.) Remove, then serve with the aïoli and a squeeze of lemon.

poached haddock, spinach and jamie's mussels

Serves 4

450g mussels in the shell
100ml single cream
4 x 200g haddock fillets
(no skin, no bone, no fear)
juice of 1 lemon
150g unsalted butter
1 onion, finely chopped
2 garlic cloves, finely chopped
900g spinach, well washed,
large stalks removed
freshly grated nutmeg
pinch of salt

This recipe was inspired by everything that's local to me in Kinsale. The haddock is caught in the harbour. Jamie harvests the mussels in Oysterhaven and the spinach is grown by Sarah in her allotment. This is a great recipe for the morning after; I've adapted it from something my father used to cook when he was feeling delicate.

In a pot, steam the mussels for two to three minutes. Strain the mussels and keep the juice. Pour the mussel juice into a pan. Add the cream and haddock and leave to simmer for six minutes. Remove the mussel meat from the shells and add to the pan with the lemon juice.

For the spinach, in a large saucepan, melt the butter, add the onion and garlic and cook for two minutes. Add the spinach, nutmeg and salt. Cook over a high heat for two minutes.

Place the spinach on warmed plates with the poached haddock on top and spoon over the creamy mussel sauce.

deep-fried tempura plaice

Serves 4

For the fish and mayonnaise
1 recipe Homemade Mayonnaise
(see page 136)
juice of 1 lemon
juice of 1 lime
vegetable oil, to deep-fry
400g plaice fillets, skinned

For the tempura batter
125g plain flour
6 tbsp cornflour
sea salt
freshly ground white pepper
250ml sparkling water

You'll have to deep-fry the plaice in batches, but that is a great excuse to enjoy your food in the most convivial manner possible, which is with everyone pitching in and helping in the kitchen, dipping the delicious fish in the citrussy mayonnaise as soon as it comes from the fryer, then getting on with the next lot.

Make the mayonnaise as on page 136, but adding the lemon and lime juice.

For the batter, mix the flour, cornflour, salt and pepper. Whisk in the sparkling water until the mixture comes together, then allow to stand for 20 minutes.

When you're ready to serve, heat the oil in a deep pan or deep-fat fryer to 190°C (375°F), (check the temperature on an oil thermometer). You shouldn't crowd the pan, but you should be able to fit about four fillets in your fryer at the same time. When the oil is ready, dip each piece of fish in the batter and place in the hot oil. Use tongs to hold the fish suspended in the oil for 30 seconds; this seals it up so it won't stick to the bottom. Then release and cook for six to eight minutes. Remove the fish, put on a plate and serve with the lemon and lime mayonnaise.

pork chops with sticky shallots, cheddar and sage mash

Serves 4

For the mash
8 spuds, peeled and chopped
sea salt
good knob of unsalted butter
generous amount of grated cheddar
10 sage leaves, finely chopped
pinch of freshly grated nutmeg
splash of milk

For the chops and shallots
16 large shallots
4 tbsp olive oil
1 sprig of thyme
4 tbsp balsamic vinegar
freshly ground black pepper
4 large pork chops

Contrary as I am, making a star of lesser ingredients has always intrigued me. I even look at turnips in soft focus, imagining their potential. This dish is made by the slow-cooked shallots, making a star out of a vegetable that is normally not allowed to shine. The rest is all about good shopping.

Preheat the oven to 180°C/350°F/gas mark and put your spuds on to boil in a very large pan of salted water.

Peel the shallots, taking care to keep their natural shape; it will help if you submerge them in warm water for 20 minutes before attacking them.

Heat the olive oil in an ovenproof frying pan and add the shallots. Allow to colour for two to three minutes, then add the thyme, balsamic vinegar, salt and pepper. Put the pan in the oven for 15 minutes, turning once or twice. The shallots should be soft and remain whole.

Cook the chops on a very hot, ridged chargrill pan for four to five minutes either side, depending on thickness. Season with salt and pepper.

Finish the potatoes: drain the spuds, then mash and add the rest of the ingredients until you have a full-flavoured, soft and creamy cloud.

Serve the mash with the chops, the shallots and their juices.

6

impressive

broad bean top and smoked bacon risotto

Serves 4

1 litre chicken stock (a cube will do)
1 sprig of thyme
100g unsalted butter
1 onion, finely chopped
8 rashers of smoked streaky bacon, finely chopped
300g arborio rice
glass of dry white wine
handful of washed broad bean tops
4 tbsp grated parmesan, plus more to serve (optional)
sea salt
freshly ground black pepper
extra virgin olive oil, to serve

While I'm waiting for the broad beans to grow in the garden, I pinch a few of the tops, taking care not to damage the plant, and make this lovely, delicate risotto. You can add the broad beans themselves, or peas or courgettes, if you like.

Bring the stock to a simmer and add the thyme.

In a heavy-based pan, melt most of the butter and add the onion and bacon. Cook gently to soften, then add the rice and stir to coat each grain with butter. Add the wine, stir until it is absorbed by the rice, then add half the stock and bring to the boil.

Allow to bubble, stirring occasionally so the rice does not stick to the pan, until the stock is nearly all absorbed, then add the remaining stock a little at a time, stirring all the time. Continue until the rice is nearly cooked, keep tasting it to check.

Add the broad bean tops, followed by the remaining butter, parmesan, salt and pepper. The consistency should be a little runny. Serve with a drizzle of extra virgin olive oil and more parmesan, if you like.

spider crab and
wild garlic risotto

Serves 4

1 onion, finely chopped
100ml olive oil
300g arborio rice
1.5 litres hot vegetable or
chicken stock
meat from 1 cooked spider crab
4 tbsp crème fraîche
12 sprigs of wild garlic, finely
chopped, plus a few wild garlic
flowers (optional, but lovely)
sea salt
freshly ground black pepper

*This may sound like a scary dish, but it's worth the effort. It takes
a while to remove the meat from the crab, and you'll need a knife, a
lobster pick, and a lot of patience, so start well in advance.*

In a large saucepan, sweat the onion in the oil over a low heat, until soft. Add
the rice and stir for two to three minutes.

Add the warm stock, little by little, constantly stirring so the rice can
absorb the stock and making sure most of it has been absorbed before adding
the next bit. This process should take about 20 minutes.

Pick through the crab meat, discarding any pieces of shell. Fold into the
risotto with the crème fraîche and wild garlic. Taste and season well, then
serve sprinkled with wild garlic flowers, if you have any.

taste of the sea: chilled seafood platter

For each person, you will need a selection of the following:

6 mussels
3 Dublin Bay prawns
1 crab claw
1 spider crab leg
50g salmon fillet
1 sardine
50g tuna steak
1 oyster
30g cooked crab meat
30g cooked, peeled prawns
50g smoked salmon

A perfect dish for the summer months. Keep an open mind when you go to the fishmonger, see what's in season, and get six or seven varieties of the fish listed left to make a beautiful platter.

If you're having mussels, Dublin Bay prawns, crab claws, spider crab legs or salmon on your platter, they'll need to be steamed. Separately steam mussels and Dublin Bay prawns for three to four minutes, crab claws and spider crab legs for seven to 10 minutes, depending on size, and salmon fillets for about five minutes, depending on size, or until just opaque all the way through.

If you're having sardines, grill the fish under a very hot grill for three to four minutes. Tuna steak will need to be seared briefly on all sides.

Serve any combination with Homemade Mayonnaise (see below), organic salad leaves, wholemeal bread and a chilled glass of white wine. You too could be in seafood heaven.

Have you ever made homemade mayonnaise? Place 2 egg yolks, a pinch of salt, 2 tsp English mustard, a pinch of cayenne pepper and 4–5 tsp white wine vinegar in a blender and process for three or four minutes. Now, with the motor running, slowly drizzle in about 350ml of groundnut oil (go very, *very* slowly at first, or the mixture may split). As the mixture begins to thicken, continue adding the oil – now in a fine, steady stream – until it has become a thick emulsion. Mix in 4 tsp of hot water to achieve a smooth consistency. Taste, and add the juice of half a lemon if you like.

It's as easy as that!

twice-baked cashel blue soufflé, beetroot and ginger relish

Serves 8

30g unsalted butter, plus a little more, melted, for the ramekins
30g plain flour
240ml hot milk
300g cashel blue cheese
4 egg yolks
6 egg whites

This is ideal for a dinner party. Sometimes the smartest thing to do is to concentrate on the main part of the dish if it's a little tricky, then serve it with your favourite shop-bought chutney, but I'm going to give you a recipe for one of my favourite chutneys, just in case you feel the need to outdo a particularly competitive friend or neighbour. The soufflés can be made the day before and kept in the fridge, as I have done for Christmas in the past.

I love having people round, but I want to join them when they are polishing off my best wine, not sweat on my own in the kitchen. By twice-baking the soufflés you can pop them in the oven when everybody is sitting down, although they will never quite have the same lustrous puff as when first taken from the oven. They will be quite delicious without you having a nervous breakdown. You will need large ramekins.

Preheat the oven to 190°C/375°F/gas mark 5. Brush eight ramekins with butter and put aside. Melt the 30g of butter in a saucepan, add the flour and cook over a low heat for three to four minutes to make a roux. Add the hot milk, a little at a time, to the roux to make a white sauce. Crumble the cheese into a large bowl and pour the sauce on top. Whisk in the yolks. Separately whisk the egg whites until stiff, then carefully fold into the cheese mixture. Fill the ramekins two-thirds full with the mixture, making sure you spoon it from the bowl from the bottom up, as the cheese tends to settle there. Place in a deep tray, then pour in hot water from the kettle to come halfway up the sides. Bake in the hot oven for 15 minutes, or until firm to the touch.

Remove from the oven and the roasting tray and allow to cool. You can make the recipe to this point the day before, then cover and refrigerate, though return to room temperature before baking for the second time.

When ready to serve, preheat the oven to 180°C/350°F/gas mark 4. Reheat the soufflés for six to seven minutes and serve with Beetroot and Ginger Relish (see below) and a green salad.

Beetroot and ginger relish. I'd use disposable kitchen gloves for this, to avoid semi-permanent crimson stains on your hands. Sweat 1 chopped onion in 1 tbsp unsalted butter until very soft, then add 3 tbsp caster sugar and season well. Add 4 large raw beetroots, peeled and grated, 125ml red wine, 30ml red wine vinegar and 2.5cm of root ginger, grated. Cook gently for 30 minutes, then leave until completely cold. Potted in a sterilised jar, this will keep for several weeks.

grilled scallops, rosscarbery black pudding, lemon and thyme dressing

Serves 2

For the dressing
1 tbsp English mustard
50g caster sugar
pinch of sea salt, or to taste
100ml rapeseed oil, plus more to
sear the black pudding and scallops
juice of 1 lemon
1 tbsp finely chopped thyme, plus a
few sprigs to serve (optional)

For the rest
2 parsnips, peeled and
finely chopped
freshly grated nutmeg
2 tbsp runny honey
30g unsalted butter
50ml single cream
1 Rosscarbery black pudding
6 hand-dived king scallops

All that's good about west Cork can be found in this dish. It's my west Cork version of surf and turf, so I've stolen some of Paul's beloved black pudding to make it! Make sure your scallops haven't been dredged, as that is disastrous for the sea bed.

To make the dressing, place the mustard, sugar and salt in a small bowl. Whisk in the 100ml of oil and the lemon juice. Season with salt and sprinkle in the thyme.

Cook the parsnips in boiling water until soft, then drain well, mash and add the nutmeg, honey, butter and cream. Keep warm.

Slice the black pudding into six rounds of a similar thickness to the scallops. Heat a frying pan over a high heat, add some oil, then, working quickly, sear the pudding and scallops for two minutes on each side.

Place the parsnip mash attractively on two warmed plates, with the black pudding and scallops on top. Drizzle the dressing over, add a sprig of thyme if you like, and serve.

saffron chicken

Serves 4

2 tbsp unsalted butter
1 tbsp vegetable oil
1 onion, finely chopped
3 garlic cloves, crushed
2.5cm piece of root ginger,
finely chopped
8 cardamom pods, crushed
¼ tsp ground cinnamon
¼ tsp chilli powder
300ml yogurt
3 tbsp ground almonds
juice of 1 lemon
sea salt
freshly ground black pepper
pinch of saffron strands
1 whole chicken, skinned
and jointed
300ml double cream
2 tbsp chopped coriander
leaves

I simply love all these flavours, and it's a one-pot dish so there is very little washing-up afterwards. I robbed the recipe from a friend who cooked it for us one evening. It's fab.

Preheat the oven to 180°C/350°F/gas mark 4.

In a large casserole, melt the butter and add the oil. Add the onion, garlic and ginger and fry over a medium heat.

Meanwhile, mix all the dry spices, yogurt, ground almonds, lemon juice, salt, pepper and saffron in a mixing bowl.

When the onion, garlic and ginger mixture is soft, pour the spice mixture into the casserole with it and cook for about one minute.

Add the chicken pieces and 300ml of water and bring to a simmer. Cover with a lid and cook in the hot oven for 30 minutes.

Remove from the oven and stir in the cream. Sprinkle with the coriander and serve with pilaf rice.

lobster, wholegrain mustard and whiskey cream

Serves 2

900g live lobster
sea salt
4 tbsp Irish whiskey
2 tbsp wholegrain mustard
200ml single cream

You haven't lived until you have tried lobster at least once. The most humane way to dispatch the beast is to plunge it into boiling water.

Plunge the lobster into heavily salted boiling water and cook for eight minutes (some say the water should be as salty as the sea). Take out and cool.

Cut in half with a heavy knife, remove the meat from the shell, discarding any black intestinal thread you find and the bony sac inside the head, and chop the meat. Crack the claws with the back of the knife and remove this meat as well. Keep the main shell to present the lobster.

For the sauce, pour the whiskey into a hot pan and quickly set alight. When the flames die down, add the mustard and cream. Bring to the boil and simmer for two minutes. Fold in the lobster meat and simmer for two minutes more, then return it to the shell. Enjoy.

grilled dover sole, anchovy and parsley butter

Serves 4

For the anchovy and parsley butter
4 tbsp finely chopped
flat-leaf parsley
8 anchovy fillets
juice of ½ lemon
200g unsalted butter

For the fish
50ml rapeseed oil
sea salt
freshly ground black pepper
4 medium dover sole

Simple, but stunning.

To make the anchovy and parsley butter, place all the ingredients in a food processor. Blend until smooth, then turn out on to a sheet of cling film or baking parchment and roll into a sausage shape, twisting the ends like a Christmas cracker. Chill for at least two hours, until firm.

Pre-heat your grill and lightly oil the grill tray. Season the fish on both sides. Grill for four to five minutes on each side, then carefully transfer to warmed plates. Slice the anchovy and parsley butter, place on top of the fish and allow to melt. This is best served simply with steamed potatoes.

chicken, lemon and tarragon croquettes

Makes about 30

30g unsalted butter
60g plain flour, plus more to coat
450ml milk, plus more to coat
sea salt
freshly ground black pepper
250g cooked chicken,
finely chopped
2 tbsp finely chopped tarragon
zest of ½ unwaxed lemon
pinch of freshly grated nutmeg
2 eggs
about 125g white breadcrumbs
vegetable oil, to deep-fry

A brilliant way to use up leftover chicken. These are perfect little tapas and great for a drinks party. You can shallow-fry them instead: just pat the croquettes flat like little fish cakes and cook in a frying pan.

Melt the butter over a gentle heat, add the flour and cook for two or three minutes. Add the milk little by little, whisking to ensure there are no lumps, then cook for two or three minutes until thick and creamy. Add the salt, pepper, chicken, tarragon, lemon zest and nutmeg. The mixture should be very thick and creamy, much more so than your normal white sauce. Cool, cover and chill for at least two hours.

Take a teaspoon of the mix and roll with your hands into an egg shape. Repeat with the rest. Lay the croquettes on a plate and chill for a little longer.

Beat the eggs with a splash of milk and pour into a broad, shallow dish. Put some flour in a second dish and season it, and place the breadcrumbs in a third dish. Line the dishes up on your work top: flour first, then egg, then breadcrumbs. (It's best if you set up a little conveyer belt system to do this.)

Roll the croquettes first in the flour, shaking off the excess, then turn through the egg and finally coat with the breadcrumbs.

Set a deep-fryer filled with vegetable oil to 170°C (340°F) and deep-fry the croquettes, in batches, until golden, keeping the cooked ones warm while you fry the rest. Serve immediately with the Creamy Dip (see below).

This *creamy dip* is lovely with the croquettes, but also makes a fantastic dressing for Cos lettuce, akin to that for a Caesar salad. Boil 2 finely chopped shallots in 1 tbsp white wine vinegar and 100ml white wine until almost dry. Remove from the heat. When cool, put 200g of fromage frais into a bowl with 100ml lightly whipped cream (or use all crème fraîche instead, if it's easier), the shallots, some chopped chives, salt and pepper. Chill until ready to serve.

duck breast in caramel with champ sauce

Serves 4 as a starter

For the champ
6 potatoes
sea salt
about 150ml milk, plus more
if needed
75g unsalted butter
freshly grated nutmeg
4 spring onions, finely chopped

For the duck and caramel
75g brown sugar
100ml sherry vinegar
1 star anise
2 big plump duck breasts, trimmed,
but skin on
freshly ground black pepper
2 tbsp sunflower oil

I've decided to do this funky little dish in bite size, but you could certainly scale it up and use one duck breast per person, if you prefer.

Boil the potatoes with a pinch of salt.

To make the caramel, put the sugar, vinegar and star anise into a pan, bring to the boil, reduce the heat and allow to reduce by one-third. Set aside.

Season the duck on the flesh side. Preheat a frying pan, add the oil and sear the duck, flesh side down, until golden, then turn the breasts skin side down. Reduce the heat and allow to cook for five minutes, then turn the duck once more and cook for a final two minutes. Remove from the heat and place between two plates, to rest.

Meanwhile, drain the potatoes and mash as finely as you can; a mouli or ricer would be perfect for this. Whip in the milk, butter, salt, pepper and nutmeg, then add the spring onions and keep warm. The champ should be a cross between a mash and a sauce; if it's too thick, add a little more milk.

To finish, put the caramel pan back over the heat and return it to a gentle boil until it gets sticky. Be very careful, as hot caramel is dangerous stuff.

Halve each duck breast lengthways, then cut them across into nuggets. Set the pieces of duck on kitchen paper and pat dry as far as possible, then toss them into the caramel and remove the pan from the heat.

Spoon the champ into small warmed bowls. Stick a cocktail stick into each piece of duck and drain off excess caramel, then nestle into the little bowls of champ sauce.

seared lamb chops, wild garlic and hazelnut risotto

Serves 4

For the chops
1 garlic clove, finely chopped
2 tbsp red wine vinegar
1 tsp smoked paprika
75ml olive oil
small pinch of caster sugar
sea salt
freshly ground black pepper
8 best end lamb chops

For the risotto
1 small onion, finely chopped
generous knob of unsalted butter
1 sprig of thyme
1 rasher of smoked bacon,
finely chopped
380g arborio rice
glug of dry cider
1 litre warm chicken stock
3 tbsp grated parmesan
2 tbsp crushed roasted hazelnuts

If you ever want something new to do with a lamb chop, this is it. Yes, I know Martin has given a wild garlic risotto too, but, hey, we filmed the show and put this book together in wild garlic season, and it's too good to miss. Besides, mine's better than his...

To marinate the chops, whisk together the garlic, vinegar, paprika, oil, sugar and seasoning in a large, shallow dish. Turn the chops in the marinade, cover with cling film and leave for at least one hour. (If you leave them for longer, all the better, but keep them in the fridge and remember to return them to room temperature before cooking.)

For the risotto, cook the onion very slowly in the butter, along with the thyme and bacon. (A wide, heavy-based saucepan or sauté pan is best for making risotto.) When soft, add the rice, stir around and add the cider. When the cider has been absorbed, add half the stock and bring to a gentle simmer, stirring occasionally so that it doesn't stick to the pan.

After about 10 minutes, the stock will have been absorbed by the rice. Keep adding the remaining stock little by little, stirring, until the rice is soft. To finish, add the parmesan and 3 tbsp of Wild Garlic Purée (see below), more if you like, then season.

Meanwhile, place a ridged cast-iron griddle pan on the heat and leave it to get smoking hot. Drain the marinade from the chops and sear them for three minutes each side. Leave to rest, off the heat, for five minutes.

Serve the risotto sprinkled with toasted hazelnuts, with the lamb chops.

Wild garlic purée is an excellent jarful to have in your fridge in April and May, to use as a condiment, with pasta, to add to sauces, or in the risotto.
Put 1 handful of washed wild garlic leaves in a liquidiser with enough light olive oil to allow the machine to turn round and process. Add salt and a little caster sugar, then blend to a smooth purée. This will keep in a sterilised jar in the fridge for up to two weeks.

poached turbot, ballycotton new potatoes, hollandaise sauce

Serves 4

For the fish and potatoes
1 onion, sliced
25ml white wine vinegar
few sprigs of parsley
6 black peppercorns
1 x 2kg whole turbot
1kg new potatoes
few sprigs of mint

For the hollandaise
2 egg yolks
1 tbsp white wine vinegar
225g unsalted butter
pinch of salt
juice of 1 lemon

Turbot is such a prime fish that it doesn't need a lot of cooking. With turbot, the simpler the better... If you can't get a whole fish, buy fillets and fry them instead, as we did for the photograph here.

For the fish, place two litres of water in a roasting tin and add the onion, vinegar, parsley and peppercorns. Bring to the boil. Reduce the heat, lower in the turbot and simmer for 20 minutes. At the same time, scrub the potatoes and cook in boiling salted water with the mint for 20 minutes, then drain.

Meanwhile, make the hollandaise. Place the egg yolks and vinegar in a bowl. Place over a pot of simmering water and whisk to a creamy consistency. Gently melt the butter in a separate pan. Remove the bowl with the egg yolks from the pot, then very slowly whisk in the melted butter, until luscious and billowing. Season with salt and lemon juice to taste.

Carefully remove the turbot from its cooking liquor, then serve, whole, with the potatoes and hollandaise.

slow-roasted pork shoulder with soft pears, cinnamon and thyme

Serves 10

2 tsp black peppercorns, cracked
2 tbsp thyme leaves
4 garlic cloves, crushed
2 tbsp sea salt
4 tbsp extra virgin olive oil
1 boneless pork shoulder (rind off)
330ml bottle pear cider
4 fresh bay leaves
2 cinnamon sticks
4 pears
4 red onions
10 potatoes

I love lesser cuts, they have always held more interest for me than the big money premium cuts. Sure, they take a little longer to cook, but they invariably taste better and are far cheaper. This takes a fair while to cook, but there's nothing for you to do, so you can go about your day while it putters away in the oven.

The night before you want this dish, take a small bowl and mix together the cracked peppercorns, thyme, garlic, salt and oil. Stir until the mixture is uniform, then rub it evenly over the pork shoulder inside and out. Wrap the pork tightly in cling film to hold the marinade against the meat, and marinate overnight in the fridge.

The next day, five hours before you want to eat, preheat the oven to 140°C/275°F/gas mark 1.

Find a big deep pot or solid roasting tray, remove the pork from the cling film and place in the pot or tray with the cider and a little extra water to create some steam. Add the bay leaves and cinnamon. Tent the pot or tray with foil, sealing the edges well, then slow-roast in the oven for four hours.

In the last half hour, peel and quarter the pears, onions and potatoes so they are in pretty much even pieces. Remove the pork from the oven and increase the oven temperature to 200°C/400°F/gas mark 6.

Remove the foil from the pork and place the pears, onions and potatoes around the meat, making sure to baste them with the porky juices.

Cook for 30 minutes more, until the meat is golden and the crackling crisp. Remove the pork and leave to rest for 20 minutes while you turn the vegetables, baste once more in the juices, and continue to cook. Skim the excess fat from the juices and serve with the pork and roast vegetables. You should be able to pull the meat apart with a spoon.

index

acknowledgements

First published in 2012 by
Quadrille Publishing Limited,
Alhambra House,
27–31 Charing Cross Road,
London WC2H 0LS

Editorial Director: Anne Furniss
Creative Director: Helen Lewis
Project Editor: Lucy Bannell
Designer: David Rowley
Photographer: Simon Wheeler
Production Director: Vincent Smith
Production Controller: James Finan

Text © 2012 Paul Flynn and
Martin Shanahan
Edited text, design and layout © 2012
Quadrille Publishing Ltd

Cataloguing in Publication Data: a catalogue
reference for this book is available from the
British Library.

ISBN 978 184949 222 5

Printed in Italy

The book to accompany Martin and Paul's
Surf & Turf is based on an RTE Television
format.

Producer: Marie Toft
Director: Rory Cobbe
Executive Producer: Colm Crowley

Thanks to Paul Flynn, my partner in this book, for his patience, for putting up with me, and for challenging me to this duel of surf versus turf.

To Marie and Rory for directing us, to Ben and Barry for filming us, to Brendan and Kieran on sound, to Dickie and Derek for all their hard work behind the scenes, and to Patricia and John in the kitchen.

To all at RTE Cork, especially Colm and Janet.

Thank you to my wife and kids, for supporting me.

And of course thanks to the country of Ireland, for her great produce.

– martin shanahan

For Máire, Ruth and Anna.

Also for all the hard-working staff at The Tannery, past and present.

Thank you RTE for making this happen. And of course to Martin Shanahan, who reminds me that simple is always best.

Simon Wheeler captured our lives and Ireland so beautifully, and I am very grateful to him for the photography.

– paul flynn

Erris Limo Hire
For the ultimate chauffeur
Driven Experience
* Stag Parties
* Hen Parties
* 21st Birthdays
* Pub Crawls
* Weddings
* All Special Occasions
Telephone: 087 2398461